Goethe and His Publishers

Goethe and His Publishers

by

Ian C. Loram

University of Kansas Press, Lawrence, 1963

TO

M. H. L.
H. V. L.

Preface

This study concerns the facts and events relating to the publication of Goethe's works.[1] Although it draws to a certain extent upon existing bibliographical material, it is based largely upon Goethe's correspondence. We may make an arbitrary division of his letters into two parts: those written directly to his publishers, and those to his friends. The value of the first group is obvious, but the picture would be far from complete without the other, because of Goethe's peculiarity of using his friends as mediators between himself and the publishers.

The history of the publication of Goethe's works is not altogether a happy one, in part because of certain traits of his character. It is a matter of record that Goethe was associated with about twenty publishers during his lifetime. Some of these associations were brief, others only indirect, while still others lasted for years, but pieced together they give a picture of Goethe the man of business and Goethe the human being. Only four of these men—Göschen, Unger, Vieweg, and Cotta—played a large enough role in Goethe's life to warrant detailed treatment in this study.

We cannot lay at his own doorstep the entire blame for Goethe's sometimes uncomfortable relationship with the publishing profession. The practices and business ethics of the German book trade as a whole influenced his reactions.[2] The publishing guild was in turn affected by the absence of legal machinery to govern its activities and protect its interests. Piracy—that is to say, the unauthorized publication of works by unscrupulous publishers—was rampant, but as far as it has

---

1. As this book was about to go to press, a dissertation by Hans-Dieter Steinhilber, "Goethe als Vertragspartner von Verlagen," was brought to my attention. Written at Hamburg in 1960, it was promptly made available to me through the kindness of Professor R. Henzler of the "Wirtschafts- und Sozialwissenschaftliche Fakultät." Steinhilber has written a sensible, and, as nearly as I can judge, accurate account. He does not, however, touch upon the young Goethe's contacts with the publishing profession, and is inclined to put most of the blame for Goethe's behavior on the publishers, a conclusion with which I do not quite agree.

2. In his dissertation, Steinhilber gives a succinct and accurate summary of these conditions as they existed in the eighteenth century.

been possible to determine, not until the last years of Goethe's life did piracy come to mean for him a menace to the future welfare of his family.

It is evident that Goethe was unconventional, to say the least, in his attitude towards the publication of his works, although in his early years, when he had little direct contact with the publishing profession, we can only point to traces of what was to develop. If his behavior, from the time of his association with Göschen onwards, cannot be classed as ideal, we must simply accept the fact that Goethe, in spite of his unquestioned genius (or perhaps because of it), had his failings. He might have turned out to be a very dull person had the human side of him been as perfect as some of his poems. If we are to understand the whole man we are forced to probe into his relations with other human beings, and if certain characteristic weaknesses appear, they must be taken into consideration in an evaluation of his character and personality.

This book is based in part on a dissertation written at Yale University in 1949. Brief sections of it have already appeared in print, and I am grateful to the editors of the following journals for permission to reproduce them, either in whole or in part: the *Germanic Review, German Life and Letters, Modern Language Notes*, the *German Quarterly*.

The Graduate Schools of Cornell University and the University of Kansas have generously assisted me with research grants toward the completion of my work.

I am indebted to those many scholars, too numerous to mention, who, through their work in the past, have made the way easier for me, but I must single out for special thanks the late Carl Schreiber. Hermann Weigand and Curt von Faber du Faur have, at one time or another, given me invaluable assistance and criticism. The Editor of the University of Kansas Press has also been unstinting in his advice. Finally I must express my deepest gratitude to my wife for her help, understanding, and unfailing good humor.

Lawrence, Kansas   I.C.L.
March, 1962

Contents

Illustrations

Die Buchhändler sind alle des Teufels,
für sie muss es eine eigene Hölle geben.

—Gespräche, May 21, 1829.

Chapter 1

Goethe's attitude toward the publication of his works and toward those who published them was sometimes puzzling and occasionally unorthodox. The discussion which follows is an attempt to present and explain the reasons for his behavior. One can best achieve this aim by showing first Goethe's feelings about the publication of his early works, including the "fugitive" poems—that is, those poems which originally appeared elsewhere than in collected editions. When these feelings are compared with the change in attitude which begins to appear about 1791, a reasonably clear picture of Goethe's publishing activities and his relationship to his publishers emerges. However, we can understand this shift only if we know the reasons for his reservations about these men, and hence we shall have to begin with his Leipzig experiences.

It was Behrisch who planted in Goethe the germs of his early distaste for seeing his works in print and his distrust of publishers. Behrisch himself disliked both printers and publishers, and, according to Goethe's description in *Dichtung und Wahrheit*,[1] made sport of them in merciless fashion. How this affected Goethe can be seen in some of the letters which he wrote home from Leipzig. He showed a definite dislike of publicity; perhaps one could call it a shyness of the public. On May 11, 1767, he wrote to his sister Cornelia, saying in connection with his plan for a drama dealing with Pharaoh's successor: "Ich würde dir ihn schicken wenn er so leserlich geschrieben wäre dass du ihn *dechiffriren* oder Horn ihn abschreiben könnte. Ich schicke dir dafür etliche andere Producktionen, die ich aber nicht gerne wollte publick werden lassen, du kannst sie guten Freunden zeigen; nur niemanden eine Abschrift davon gegeben."[2]

1

On October 12, 1767, he wrote again to Cornelia, asking her to tell his friend Brevillière that he would receive a copy of *Die Mitschuldigen* as soon as it was finished, and that he could do what he liked with it. He complained that although he had taken to Leipzig most of his early compositions, some of them which had remained in the hands of friends were causing him trouble. "Die eine spielen die guten Leute, und machen sich und mich lächerlich, die andre drucken sie mir in eine vermaledeyte Wochenschrifft, und noch dazu mit dem J. W. G. Ich hätte mögen toll darüber werden.

"Ich schickte euch gern die Annette wenn ich nicht befürchten müsste dass ihr mir sie abschriebt. Denn auch sogar das Büchelgen das ich sosehr ausgeputzt und verbessert habe, wollte ich niemanden communicirt haben. Bishierher hat es zwölf Leser und zwo Leserinnen gehabt, und nun ist mein Publicum aus. Ich liebe gar den Lärm nicht."

Here one sees Behrisch at work, but there is yet another factor which undoubtedly strengthened the ideas which he had put into Goethe's head. On his trip from Frankfurt to Leipzig one of his fellow passengers was a publisher named Fleischer, whom he knew personally. After Goethe had completed *Die Mitschuldigen* he offered it to Fleischer for publication, but it was rejected.[3] This was naturally a disappointment to the young man, and perhaps made him feel that Behrisch was not wrong after all.

As far as it has been possible to ascertain, the contact with Fleischer was the only direct experience the young Goethe had with the publishing profession while in Leipzig. However, his association with the Breitkopf family undoubtedly gave him some insight, in a rather more informal and indirect fashion, into the field. Breitkopf himself had for years been collecting material for a history of printing and was considered an authority on the subject, so that it is likely that before Goethe left Leipzig he had absorbed a good deal of miscellaneous information which later acted in a formative fashion on his own thinking.[4]

From his correspondence it soon becomes apparent that he

had no fixed policy regarding the publication of his work. He asked often in his letters when he was enclosing something which he had just written that the addressee be sure not to let anyone make a copy of the enclosure. This is especially noticeable after his return from Leipzig, though there are many instances when he said nothing about copying or else seemed to care little about what happened to his manuscripts. There were reasons why any author of the 18th century did not want to have copies of his manuscripts drifting about where he had no control over them. One was fear of the book pirate, the *Nachdrucker*. There were some small concerns which existed solely by pirating, and several of the largest houses in Europe published without the consent or knowledge of the author.[5] The only way author and publisher could protect themselves was to obtain "privileges" from the state, but this was not always easy to do, and even "privileges" could not prevent a publisher in any other state from pirating a work as soon as it appeared.

In his early years Goethe seemed little concerned about such pirating. Not until he negotiated with Göschen in 1787 for the first edition of his collected works did it seem to have made any real impression on him. He knew, of course, that his material was being illegally reprinted, but showed what one might call an almost admirable nonchalance. There are some possible reasons for this attitude. Goethe at this early stage of his career was not dependent upon his pen for his bread and butter. He did not expect to make any substantial financial gains by the publication of an odd poem here and there, nor, if we can believe a statement he made in a letter to Sophie von La Roche of December 23, 1774, did he at that time see future monetary rewards from his writing. He may perhaps have hoped to make a little, particularly on *Götz von Berlichingen,* but did not seem to be disappointed by his lack of success. He wrote to Frau La Roche as follows: "Ich mag gar nicht daran dencken was man für seine Sachen kriegt. Und doch sind die Buchhändler vielleicht auch nicht in Schuld. Mir hat meine Autorschafft die Suppen noch nicht fett gemacht, und wirds und solls auch nicht thun." Here it seems that his dislike of bookmen was not nearly as strong as it had been, but one still cannot postulate any definite attitude. As we have indicated, a fear of piracy can hardly have been the reason for the many admonitions in his letters. One might claim that Goethe felt that his work was too good for the public, for both at this early stage and later he rarely had anything complimentary to say about his readers. Writing to Jacobi on August 21, 1774, he referred to the public as "Gaffer und Schwäzzer." And yet the impression remains, from his early letters, that he often distributed his poems in a decidedly free-handed manner. Sometimes he intended them for publication, sometimes he sent them to friends merely because he felt that they would be interested, and one cannot help thinking that sometimes he sent them simply because he was proud of them. Any number of letters to Boie, Jacobi, Merck, Auguste von Stolberg, and others contain remarks which bear this out, and illustrate the casualness and carelessness with which Goethe treated his youthful effusions. For instance, in the letter to Jacobi of August 21, 1774, he said: "Du kriegst bald kleine Sachen von mir wie ich sie finde, es liegt allerley hier und da." He showed the same inconsistency about the exact text of the early poems written for publication, telling Jacobi on December 1, 1774, that he could punctuate as he saw fit some verses submitted to *Iris,* whereas a few months earlier he had informed Salzmann that no one was going to change a single letter in any of his works. He simply did not know his own mind.[6]

These were formative years for Goethe, years too of "Sturm und Drang." He was not planning to become a great poet; he wanted to live and live as fully as possible. If one way of expressing himself was to write poems, how could he stop living long enough to worry about the fate of these children of his? He did not know what he wanted to make of his life, and it is to be doubted that he had any real worries. Being consistent was just not part of his character in his early years.

It was perhaps inconsistency which marked the method of publication of Goethe's first major work, a method which very nearly repeated itself in his last important publishing venture—Goethe as his own publisher. Towards the end of 1771 he had completed the first draft of his *Geschichte Gottfriedens von Berlichingen, dramatisiert,* and had sent it in 1772 to Herder. From November until December of 1772 Goethe was visiting Merck in Darmstadt, and probably during this period the two friends conceived the plan for their joint publication of *Götz.*[7] For some time Goethe apparently could not seriously apply himself to the task of revising the original, but a visit from Merck in February of 1773 convinced him that he had better bestir himself. By May the completed manuscript must have been in the hands of the printer, and by the middle of June Goethe was able to send a copy to Kestner.

There is nothing in Goethe's correspondence to indicate how he arranged with Merck for the printing of *Götz* or what his ideas were about publication. Only in *Dichtung und Wahrheit* do we find out what happened. From what Goethe says here, he was not particularly anxious to have the play published—he regarded it highly and did not care to go through a repetition of his experience with Fleischer in Leipzig. At this point Merck was of assistance. With his knowledge of conditions in the publishing world he felt that it would be profitable for Goethe and himself to be their own publishers. Goethe tells us that they agreed that he should provide the paper, while Merck took care of the printing. "Genug, es ward ausgemacht, dass ich das Papier anschaffen, er aber für den Druck sorgen solle; und somit ging es frisch an's Werk, und mir gefiel es gar nicht übel, meine wilde dramatische Skizze nach und nach in saubern Aushängebogen zu sehen: sie nahm sich wirklich reinlicher aus, als ich selbst gedacht."

In actuality things did not proceed nearly as smoothly as Goethe recalls in his autobiography. A combination of poor business sense and a clever and unscrupulous pirate publisher did him no good whatsoever. Still wary of bookdealers, he would have nothing to do with them, but distributed copies of the book himself to friends and asked them to dispose of them. On July 11, 1773, he wrote to Sophie von La Roche: "Mercken würden Sie einen Gefallen thun, denn er ist auch hier Verleger, wenn Sie beykommende Exemplare, sind 24 vor 48 Xr. [Kreuzer] das Stück absezzen liessen." To Kestner and Charlotte he sent a request a few days later, asking them if they would also act as booksellers, since he did not wish to entrust the sale to a professional.

The fact that Merck was in St. Petersburg at the time was unfortunate—his keen business acumen would have been of invaluable assistance. The first edition was devoured by the public,[8] and without Merck at hand Goethe was hard put to know how to meet the demand for a second. He found himself unable to bear the financial burden of another edition; in fact, it was not until much later that he was able to pay for the paper required for the first.[9] The result was that an unscrupulous publisher seized upon the opportunity to issue a pirated edition, very poorly done and full of misprints.[10]

Goethe's reaction to the pirating was typical of his still nonchalant attitude towards the distribution and eventual fate of his work. Writing to Boie on January 8, 1774, he asked for his assistance, saying that he himself was no businessman, and continuing: "Ich lache manchmal drüber, wie gut das Stück aufgenommen, wie schnell verkaufft, nachgedruckt worden und ich die Druckerkosten noch nicht einmal wieder habe."

In May, 1773, Goethe wrote to Kestner, asking him to tell Kielmansegge that *Fingal,* the first part of the Merck-Goethe publication of an English version of Ossian's work, had been printed and was selling for 36 Kreuzer.[11] On May 12 he sent Sophie von La Roche twelve copies. Whether she was expected to sell them or distribute them as complimentary copies Goethe did not say, but in view of the manner in which *Götz* was sold it is quite possible that she was to act as agent, taking the place of a bookdealer. These brief statements are all that Goethe had to say about the second product of his venture into publishing. We may assume that it was a failure, since two volumes were all that appeared until 1777, when Fleischer in Leipzig issued the last two.

We see then that neither of Goethe's early experiments as his own publisher was successful. Apparently he learned his lesson, because it was not until fifty years later that he again seriously considered the idea when he was preparing the *Ausgabe letzter Hand* for publication. He went so far as to say that he was not cut out to be a businessman, although in later years he was usually loath to admit it.

About the publication of two other early works, *Zwo wichtige . . . Biblische Fragen* and *Brief des Pastors . . .* we know virtually nothing.[12]

In 1774, about the time when Goethe had finished writing his *Jahrmarktsfest zu Plundersweilern,* his friend Klinger found himself in very straitened circumstances.[13] Goethe, in a burst of generosity, gave Klinger the manuscript and told him to have it published, saying that he could retain all the profits. In the course of the summer Klinger, who was studying at Giessen, decided to avail himself of Goethe's offer and asked Höpfner, a professor of law, to help him find a publisher. Höpfner thought immediately of Nicolai, and wrote asking whether he would be interested, assuring him that no personal satires were involved.[14] On July 14, having received no reply, Höpfner wrote again to Nicolai, telling him that more manuscripts were available, and urging a prompt reply, since their owner needed money badly.[15] Nicolai finally answered Höpfner, rejecting his offer in a rather sharp letter, the tone of which indicates that he was not sympathetic towards anything in which Goethe had a part. He was afraid of publishing that which he was sure smacked of personal satire, in spite of Höpfner's assurances. As a result, either Höpfner or Goethe himself approached Weygand in Leipzig, and in 1774 there appeared *Neueröffnetes moralischpolitisches Puppenspiel,* containing *Prolog, Künstlers Erdenwallen, Jahrmarktsfest zu Plundersweilern,* and *Pater Brey.*

This episode has been treated in some detail because it is important both for the history of the publication of one of

Goethe's works, and because it brings to light again a specific characteristic of the young man—a sort of careless but well-meaning generosity, that resulted in a gesture arising partly out of sympathy for a friend, and partly out of a feeling that if there was anything of which he had an excess and could afford to give away, it was some of his writing in one form or another. Besides, an offer of money might have offended Klinger; a manuscript was apparently acceptable.

In connection with the authorized publication by a friend of one of his works, it is interesting to note here Goethe's reaction to another publication, also by a friend, of one of his early pieces—namely, *Götter, Helden und Wieland,* which Lenz had published in Kehl in March of 1774. Lenz himself said of his action, writing to Wieland seven years later: "Ich liess Götter, Helden und Wieland drucken, und ohne mich hätten sie das Tageslicht nimmer gesehen."[16] This statement might indicate that Lenz acted without Goethe's permission, although in *Dichtung und Wahrheit* the latter wrote that he gave in to Lenz's insistence that it be published. Only later, said Goethe, did he discover that this was one of Lenz's first moves to harm and discredit him in the eyes of the public.[17] It is very possible that this episode may have had something to do with Goethe's frequent requests to friends not to make copies of his work, so that they should not get into the hands of impulsive people like Lenz, who would have them published.

As we have seen, Goethe was considerably in debt following the publication of *Götz.* On June 22, 1774, he wrote Boie that he was planning to publish *Werther* and *Clavigo.* The question which enters one's mind here is whether Goethe had any idea of publishing *Werther* when he wrote it, in order perhaps to pay off his debts, or whether, as he claims, he decided on publication because Merck pressed the point. He wrote in *Dichtung und Wahrheit* that after the decision to publish had been made, a letter from Weygand in Leipzig arrived on the day of Cornelia Goethe's marriage to Schlosser, asking Goethe for a manuscript for publication. This combination of circumstances he considered a favorable omen, sent the *Werther* off to Leipzig, and was pleasantly surprised that the remuneration was not entirely swallowed up by the debts incurred over *Götz*.[18]

Interesting to note here is the fact that although there were several pirated editions of *Werther,* Goethe, in his correspondence of the period, makes no mention of them whatsoever. Nor does he have anything to say about the fact that Weygand, the publisher of the authorized first edition, pirated it in 1787.

The facts about the conception and the writing of *Clavigo* are given us by Goethe in *Dichtung und Wahrheit,* but as far as the publication of it is concerned, we are left very much in the dark. One noteworthy point about *Clavigo* is that it was the first important work of Goethe's to appear under his name. Hitherto the major works of the early period had appeared anonymously. Why Goethe suddenly decided to have his name on the title-page has never been satisfactorily explained. All that we can do is to pose further questions. Was he proud of what he had written? Had he, therefore, overcome his shyness of the public? Or is this simply another example of his youthful inconsistency?

Although *Satyros* was not published until 1817, Goethe may have had thoughts of making it public prior to that date. Our information is rather unreliable and contradictory. For instance, on May 28, 1774, Goethe sent the manuscript to Klopstock, saying that it would probably never be printed and asking for its quick return. About a month later, on June 23, 1774, Zimmermann wrote to Lavater that he had met a very pleasant chap who told him that Goethe was about to publish a farce.[19] Since nothing is known about Zimmermann's informant, one must admit that the evidence is inconclusive.

Goethe himself had nothing enlightening to say about the *Prolog zu den neusten Offenbarungen Gottes,* but there is a clue in a letter from Höpfner to Nicolai of March 14, 1774. Höpfner told the publisher that it had been printed in Darmstadt, but the title-page gives Giessen. Morris' theory is that

Giessen is used to indicate Bahrdt's home as the scene of the action, rather than the place of publication.[20] If Höpfner was correct, then probably the *Prolog* was published by Merck and Goethe even as *Götz* had been, since Darmstadt was Merck's home.

Stella, although not printed until after Goethe had reached Weimar, he had nevertheless written before leaving Frankfurt. On March 6, 1775, he sent Johanna Fahlmer the first sheets, telling her to copy them off if they amused her. And on August 3, he told Lavater to send *Stella* to Lenz immediately. One would think that after the experience he had had with Lenz and the publication of *Götter, Helden und Wieland* only a year before he would have been a little more cautious about sending unpublished manuscripts to him. If Lenz ever received the manuscript he was apparently more prudent than before, since we know nothing of his having anything to do with its publication.

As far as we know, the publication of *Stella* was the first real instance of Goethe's approaching a publisher through an intermediary, in this case Merck. Being his own publisher had proved too difficult. More interesting, however, is the fact that Goethe, even at this early age, was well aware of his own worth and laid down conditions under which Mylius could have his *Stella,* similar to those which he stipulated to Vieweg for *Hermann und Dorothea* many years later; that is to say, Goethe wanted a fixed sum (20 taler) for the manuscript, sight unseen. Mylius took a rather sensible attitude towards the conceited young author, in his letter of October 24, 1775, to Merck: "Es ist allerdings wohl Eigensinn vom Hrn. Dr. *Göthe,* wenn er seine *Msc.* auf die Art verkaufen will; denn unter uns gesagt, es ist etwas sonderbar, unbesehen und, nach dem alten Sprüchwort, die Katze im Sack zu kaufen. Auch ist mit einer so kleinen Pièce ja kein grosser Handel zu machen." He went on to say that he was willing to take a chance and pay Goethe what he demanded for *Stella,* principally because he wanted to establish contact with such a prolific young author. He hoped that his willingness to co-operate would not have the opposite effect from that which he expected. He explained this by saying: "Denn da er nun für diese vielleicht kleine und nicht so sehr interessante Piece 20 Thlr. bekommt, so wird das folgende Stück 50 Thlr. und Dr. Faust vielleicht 100 Louis d'or gelten sollen; das ist aber wider die Natur der Sache und nicht auszuhalten, und ich thue von ganzem Herzen Verzicht darauf. Mich wundert übrigens, dass der Herr Dr. *Göthe* die Buchhändler so quälen will, da er, wie ich immer gehört habe, solches aus öconomischen Gründen nicht nöthig hat. Soll es also vielleicht Ruhm seyn, dass ihm seine *Msc.* so theuer sind bezahlt worden?"[21]

Mylius, obviously a man of some experience, showed the regrettable tendency of many publishers of the day to pay very little for what he published. It was only natural that an author, if he found himself successful, should expect more for his work as he matured, but Mylius was unwilling to gratify such expectations. Goethe already had a reputation, as Mylius admitted. To be sure, he may have looked upon Goethe as a dilettante in the world of letters; we can perhaps forgive him for this, since even Goethe himself did not foresee that he would at a later date depend largely upon his pen for a comfortable living. One wonders what Mylius would have thought of Goethe's demands upon Vieweg.

This little episode is actually the earliest illustration of a side of Goethe's character which was to play an important part in his association with almost all his later publishers. It is an indication of his growing conviction that he had something good to offer the public but that how it appeared was not entirely his concern. He had produced it; those persons whose task it was to see that it was made public could know nothing of the processes by which it was produced, and hence were not worthy of the author's consideration.

Goethe showed similar unconcern about his *Singspiele*. The fact that they were written for a relatively small circle indicates that he was really not concerned whether they were made public or not. *Erwin und Elmire* had appeared in

Jacobi's *Iris* in Düsseldorf in 1775, before Goethe's journey to Weimar. In the case of *Claudine von Villa Bella,* we know virtually nothing except that it was published by Mylius in 1776. Goethe was apparently concerned about its appearing in an unauthorized edition, for on June 4 he sent the manuscript to Knebel with the plea not to copy it under any circumstances. When Knebel delayed the return of the manuscript for almost two months, Goethe wrote on August 1 demanding to have it back. In 1780 the songs from *Jery und Bätely* appeared in Weimar, probably published by Glüsing, a local publisher of little importance. The work in its entirety came out in 1790, as part of the Göschen edition. *Die Fischerin* was published in 1782 by Glüsing. Worth noting is the fact that Anna Amalia paid for this venture. Publication of *Die Vögel* in 1787 and *Scherz, List und Rache* in 1790 was undertaken by Göschen, as part of Goethe's collected works.

At the beginning of the Weimar period, Goethe showed the same carefree, almost careless, attitude, but there were some indications that he was beginning to think more consistently about making his work public. It is far more difficult now to trace Goethe's feelings for the reason that he published so little until 1785. In general, however, his thoughts about publishing were much the same as they had been before his arrival in Weimar. Even the publication of the first authorized edition of his collected works by Göschen was not brought about by any genuine desire on Goethe's part, such as we shall find later on, to see his works in print. Rather it was motivated by financial reasons.

Goethe's first literary publications after moving to Weimar were again scattered poems in various books and journals. During the period 1775-1790 he published thirty-two poems, eighteen of them in 1776. Probably half of these had been written before he left Frankfurt, and their importance for this study is limited solely to indications that he was beginning to realize that there should be some purpose to his publications. Three of these poems appeared in 1776 in the German translation of Mercier's *Du Théâtre ou nouvel essai sur l'art dramatique.*[22] Goethe was supposed to contribute notes and poems to this volume, but the notes never appeared. However, we do find an introduction by him to the appendix of the book which throws some light on his thinking: "Folgende Blätter streu ich ins Publikum mit der Hoffnung, dass sie die Menschen finden werden, denen sie Freude machen können. Sie enthalten Bemerkungen und Grillen des Augenblicks, meist über bildende Kunst, und scheinen also hier am unrechten Platz hingeworfen. Sey's also nur denen, die einen Sprung über die Gräben, wodurch Kunst von Kunst gesondert wird, als *salto mortale* nicht fürchten, und solchen, die mit freundlichem Herzen aufnehmen, was man ihnen in harmloser Zutraulichkeit hinreicht. So auch mit den Gedichten."[23]

The phrase "streu ich ins Publikum" is reminiscent of the very young Goethe carelessly tossing odd pages of material about without much concern as to where they might land, but the very fact that he bothered to write the introduction at all, giving an explanation of why this appendix was included, is significant, since it shows the first signs—faint as they may be—of a dawning consciousness that he was publishing something with a purpose in mind. He seemed to feel here that perhaps he had something which would benefit others.

In an anonymous collection of songs published in 1777 there appeared four poems from *Erwin und Elmire*.[24] Goethe had offered the publisher Reich a small volume of his poems set to music by Kayser shortly before the appearance of this collection, and possibly the anonymous edition contained some of those which Goethe mentioned in his letter to Reich. Why he went so far as to approach Reich is hard to say, but he had dealt with him before, acting as mediator for Lavater, and he may have felt that Reich was to be trusted. The tone of this letter of April 28, 1777, seems to indicate a certain maturity on Goethe's part, a departure from the headlong, impulsive Goethe whom we have known so far, a tendency, even though it is slight, toward reflection and consideration.

If the number of poems appearing in these years seems

very small in comparison with what Goethe had composed earlier, we must bear in mind that the *Italienische Reise* fell in this period, and that the pressure of official duties was very great. Add to this the fact that *Iphigenie, Tasso,* and the various *Singspiele* were completed and that Goethe wrote *Wilhelm Meisters Theatralische Sendung* at this time, and we can see why he would have little leisure for other accomplishments. Most important of all perhaps, was his preoccupation, during the years 1786-1790, with Göschen and the publication of the first authorized edition of his collected works.

The decision to authorize the publication of his collected works by Georg Joachim Göschen was his first real appearance before the public following the phenomenal success of *Götz* and *Werther,* and when, writing in his diary on January 19, 1780, he called Friedrich Justin Bertuch "entsetzlich behaglicher Laps" it probably did not enter his mind that Bertuch would one day be instrumental in negotiating the publication of this edition. Bertuch was involved in numerous ventures in and around Weimar, and when it came to organizing or starting a new project, Bertuch was the man to see, since he knew practically everybody. What was important for Goethe was that he knew Georg Joachim Göschen, a young and comparatively inexperienced Leipzig publisher, who was trying to build up his new business.

The exact date is not known, but some time in the first half of 1786 preliminary arrangements were being made by the ubiquitous Bertuch to have Göschen publish Goethe's collected works. From the small amount of correspondence between Göschen and Bertuch which is available, it is quite apparent that the latter was actually far more than a mere intermediary between Goethe and his publisher. The pronoun "we" appears often, and Bertuch had gone so far as to put up a certain amount of capital to back this, Göschen's greatest venture to date.[25] One can look upon them almost as partners, which would account for the sometimes conspiratorial tone of their correspondence. Goethe apparently was unaware of this partnership.

The reasons for Göschen's desire to have Goethe on his list of authors are fairly obvious. To any young man, the right to publish the works—particularly the first authorized edition—of a writer whose name had become almost a household word in Germany would be the best sort of publicity he could obtain. It would help to an incalculable degree to put a young and struggling enterprise upon a firmer basis, and this accounts almost entirely for Göschen's agreement to Goethe's terms. Had he foreseen the trials and tribulations which lay ahead, he might have been less anxious to enter into a contract with him.

Goethe's reasons for negotiating with Göschen are not quite so clear. There are some, other than those he gave to Göschen, which we can work out for ourselves, the most important being that he had published relatively little in the first ten years of his stay in Weimar. Goethe, apart from his early years, often had a difficult time writing. In many instances it was apparently a case of driving himself, forcing himself to sit down and put words on paper—except when he wrote to Frau von Stein. True, he had written *Wilhelm Meisters Theatralische Sendung* and the *Singspiele,* but the latter are slight in substance, having been composed for the most part to please the court circle, and he was beginning to feel that if he were obligated to publish, he might be able to complete some of the more important works which at the time were only fragments.

He had finally begun to think seriously of the dangers of piracy, and realized that by having an authorized edition of his works issued he would in some measure restrict the activities of men like Himburg, who had already issued three pirated editions of the works. More important to him, perhaps, was the plan which had finally matured in his mind to spend some time in Italy. This required more money than he had at hand, and although Carl August granted him leave of absence with pay, there was no telling how expensive the trip would be, or how long he was to be away from Weimar.

The beginning of the negotiations with Göschen, with

Bertuch's assistance, were probably largely oral, so that it is not until the end of June 1786 that we come across a note to Bertuch which gives us a definite starting point. At that time Goethe told Bertuch that he was sending him a tentative draft of his public notification of intention to publish and asked for his assistance in editing it.

In this public notice he gave two important reasons for his desire to see his collected works in print, first, the continuing danger of piracy, and second, the fact that manuscripts sent to friends were gradually finding their way into print. He went on to say that since he could not offer a large quantity of material, he had always wished to emphasize quality, and that he had long hoped to be able to complete several fragments in the right kind of mood. But this had been, he added, a pious wish, and now only an unpleasant necessity had driven him to the decision to publish.[26]

There was a certain amount of discussion and correspondence as to payment, and although Göschen and Bertuch argued at first, they yielded because they were anxious to make sure of Goethe. His first terms were 3 louis d'or per sheet, which Göschen and Bertuch thought exorbitant.[27] Then Goethe, who did not want to be bothered calculating the number of sheets, set as his price the lump sum of 2,000 taler, which upset Bertuch even more, as can be seen from his letter to Göschen on June 29, 1786:

Ich war am Dienstage bei Göthe, und sprach mit ihm über seine Erklärung. 'Sie haben die Schraube sehr scharf angezogen', sagte ich ihm; 'Göschen wird zucken; indessen wir wollen sehn was er drauf sagt; einige Milderung werden Sie ihm auf alle Fälle accordiren müssen.' 'Es ist wahr', sagte er, 'ich habe meine Forderung etwas gesteigert, meine gedruckten und ungedruckten Werke in eine Brühe geworfen, und eine Summe überhaupt gefordert, 1. weil ihm beyde wegen der neuen Bearbeitung gleich, und so gut wie ganz neu sind; 2. um uns nicht wegen den diversen Bogen Berechnung zu geniren; 3. weil ich, da Göschen nicht changirt, sondern bloss coulant handelt, auf eine *2te Auflage* so gut als nicht rechne, und also alles was ich hoffen kann von dieser erwarten muss. Hingegen will ich ihn wegen der Stärke der Auflage gar nicht einschränken, und für die gute Auflage in gr. 8 vo. auch nichts verlangen; auch die Subscription auf alle Art durch meine Freunde unterstützen helfen, etc. etc.[28]

The two partners, in spite of Bertuch's complaints, hardly put up more than a token resistance, so that on July 6 Goethe could tell Charlotte von Stein he had come to an agreement with Göschen, giving in on only one point. He sounded very pleased with himself here, as though he was proud of his ability to drive a hard bargain.

This same letter brings up an interesting point. We begin to see how Goethe, either by virtue of his magnetic personality or because of his reputation as an author, had very little difficulty in getting his friends to perform many of the more routine chores when it came to a venture such as this publication. He told Charlotte that Wieland and Herder were already going over his works very thoroughly. Because of Wieland's assistance, Goethe felt it would be easy to work the first four volumes into the final revised form, but he admitted that the last four would cost him a certain amount of effort. From the generally calm tone in which he expressed himself, it is doubtful whether he realized just how much trouble they would really be.

While this was going on in Weimar, Göschen was not being idle in Leipzig. For a man who was anxious to make a good beginning, he was taking quite a risk and being not a little underhanded. He decided not to publish an edition in large format. He also planned to print 3,000 more copies than there were subscribers, who numbered about 1,000. Thus there would be a regular edition of 4,000 copies and a cheaper one of 2,000. He said that he would not mention this to Goethe until the time was ripe.[29]

Meantime, knowing nothing of what was being planned in Leipzig, Goethe was beginning to discover that the publication of one's collected works, even in eight rather slender volumes, was not an easy task, but he went to work, and apparently spent a large part of the next month at his revision,

17

driven by the thought that he simply had to get away from Weimar as soon as possible. He realized what a task he had undertaken after he had worked the first four volumes into final form, and at the start of his Italian journey wrote to Carl August on September 2 saying that he had taken the whole thing too lightly. To do his task properly he would be forced to lose himself in a part of the world where he was unknown, and where he could find the necessary leisure and proper atmosphere. Goethe's intentions were the best, but there were more important reasons for his journey to Italy; and as we shall see, only when he thought of what he was duty-bound to do in order not to prolong publication could he force himself to make much progress.

While still in Carlsbad he wrote a long letter to Göschen on September 2. We do not know what Göschen's first reaction was, but as a solid, conventional businessman, he would have been upset, particularly if he had thought that the letter was typical of Goethe's business methods. Unless Bertuch had informed Göschen that Goethe was planning a trip to Italy, this was the first that he had heard about it. Goethe told him that he had "eine kleine Reise" in mind and that he was not just sure when he would return.[30] He informed Göschen that he had the first and second volumes ready, and would deliver them upon receipt of one quarter of the money which was stipulated in the contract. This rather unusual stipulation is one with which we shall become much more familiar, since it was a condition which Goethe frequently insisted upon; one which almost caused Cotta to sever relations with him some forty-three years later. Goethe stated in a rather cavalier fashion that the next two volumes could be delivered to Göschen by or shortly after Michaelmas, and that it was quite possible that Göschen would not need them even then. Until Easter they had sufficient time to think about the last four volumes. He went on to say that he did not want the fragments to remain as such, and would do his utmost to complete them. Then came a remark which is most inconsistent with his behavior later on: "Ich lege verschiedene Bemerckungen hier bey, die Bezug auf den Druck haben, machen Sie davon beliebigen Gebrauch, ein kluger Korrektor muss am Ende doch das beste thun."[31] If Göschen had been better acquainted with Goethe, he would have followed every single instruction to the letter, since we shall see how, all through Goethe's relationships with his publishers, he gave specific instructions and for the most part insisted on their execution. For Goethe there was rarely such a thing as allowing a publisher to use his own judgment.

For the time being, everything seemed to be proceeding according to plan. Göschen had succeeded in attaining one of the objects of a trip to Vienna, namely, protection from having this edition pirated in Austria.[32] In October he received the first two volumes from Goethe's secretary Seidel in return for the 500 taler which Goethe had demanded. In October Goethe was still working on *Iphigenie* for the third volume and *Stella* for the fourth, but he was not in the least worried and wrote naïvely to Seidel on October 14 that there was no great hurry, since the printing of the other volumes would keep Göschen occupied.

Göschen now began to find himself plagued by two things, Goethe's dilatoriness and the distance between Rome and Leipzig. On October 22, he wrote anxiously to Bertuch because Goethe had not yet let him know the subjects for the illustrations.[33] If the matter was not settled very soon, the artist, Chodowiecki, would tire of waiting and accept some other commission. This would then put Göschen in the awkward position of either having to break his word to his readers and issue the volumes without the promised illustrations, or of having to find some less skilled illustrator to do a hurried job at the last minute. Göschen was also worried because, in spite of Goethe's instructions that Herder was to act for him, he was not sure whether Herder and Goethe would see eye to eye on specimen pages which were being set up.[34] And now, after the contract had been signed and work had begun, Göschen began to show signs of anxiety about the completion of some of the fragments. It seems peculiar that he should not

19

have previously considered the possibility that he might run into trouble on this point, but perhaps he was overanxious to pin Goethe down to a contract. In spite of the difficulties he could nevertheless appreciate Goethe's worth as a writer, and told Bertuch in December: "Der ganze Mann ist doch Genie."[35]

The following month, January 1787, Goethe had still given Göschen no inkling as to what was in his mind, or how much progress he was making. Some of Göschen's fears had materialized, since both Chodowiecki and Meil had in the meantime accepted other illustrating commissions, and yet he was still able to say that progress had been made and that *Werther* was in press. From a letter to Herder of December 2, 1786, we know, however, that Goethe was busy with *Iphigenie* in Rome and appeared quite optimistic about completing it in the near future, although he too was beginning to realize what a task he had undertaken.

He was keeping a sharp eye on the financial side of their arrangement, as we can see from a letter to Seidel of January 13, asking for reports on Göschen's payments. He emphasized again in this letter the fact that he was determined to live up to the terms of the contract, at least as far as the completion of the fragments was concerned. But in spite of his serious concentration on *Iphigenie,* he was nevertheless fearful of how Italy might affect his wishes to give the final touch to the remaining works. Writing to Kayser on January 13 about the distractions with which he was beset, he said: "Ich brauche dazu viel Geduld und Zusammennehmens, in einer fremden Welt wo mich alles aus mir herauszieht und mich an sich lockt." At the very time when he felt that by obligating himself to a publisher he could make himself write, he plunged into a life which offered everything detrimental to that resolution.

In spite of the dearth of letters from Goethe, Göschen had not lost faith and was determined to get along with him, but he was disturbed over the apparent coolness of the public

Georg Joachim Göschen. Artist unknown.

Johann Friedrich Unger. Artist unknown. Courtesy
of the Yale University Library.

towards the announcement of the forthcoming edition.[36] Goethe could not share his worries.

On February 20, Goethe assumed that Göschen had received the first four volumes complete and wrote that he was busy reworking the material for the last four. He was at the moment occupied with *Tasso* and hoped to have two more volumes ready in the fall. "Das Publikum wird gerne warten," he said. "Wenigstens habe ich von allen Enden her Zuruf dass ich die Stücke endigen soll." In view of the public's lack of interest, it is quite obvious that Goethe had no inkling of the situation, or that he was thinking solely of the relatively small group of friends and admirers who were urging him to bring his works to completion. So inspiring did he feel this sojourn in Italy was going to be that he suggested in this same letter to Göschen that the size of the edition might well be increased to ten volumes.

Göschen was reassured, but his peace of mind was not long-lived. In May 1787, the first three volumes of the works were offered to the general public, but—and here Göschen made a great mistake—he did not send Goethe his complimentary copies since he was hoping to provide better illustrations for them. Hence the books reached the public long before Goethe laid eyes on them. The unfortunate publisher was also being subjected to adverse comments from Weimar, where Herder, having received a copy of the first three volumes, remarked that he did not care for the printing. We can sympathize with Göschen's reaction when we remember that Herder had already approved the sample pages which had been submitted to him. "Wie soll mans am Ende in der Welt machen?" asked the publisher. "Gott weiss es, ich nicht!"[37]

On August 15, Goethe finally answered Göschen's letters of March 22 and June 5, in one of which, probably the latter, Göschen must have informed him that he was holding back the complimentary copies. Goethe showed little understanding for his publisher's position. One can see why he was irritated because he had not yet received his copies. But if we consider that Göschen held them back simply because he wished to make sure that Goethe would be pleased with them, then it seems as though the latter was adopting a rather unreasonable attitude. Compared with the next letter to Göschen, however, written on October 27, after he received his copies, his earlier remarks are mild. Goethe wrote as follows:

Ich kann nicht sagen dass der Anblick der drey Exemplare meiner Schriften . . . mir grosses Vergnügen verursacht hätte. Das Papier scheint eher gutes Druckpapier als Schreibpapier, das Format schwindet beym Beschneiden gar sehr zusammen, die Lettern scheinen stumpf, die Farbe ist wie das Papier ungleich, so dass diese Bände eher einer ephemeren Zeitschrift als einem Buch ähnlich sehen, das doch einige Zeit dauren sollte. Von ohngefähr war ein Exemplar der Himburgischen Ausgabe hier, welches gegen jene wie einem Dedikations Exemplar ähnlich sah. Diess ist nun aber geschehen und nicht zu redressiren. Auch finde ich in einigen Stücken, die ich durchlaufen, Druckfehler und Auslassungen, kann aber nicht entscheiden, ob es am Manuscripte oder am Correcktor liege.

Göschen, who was probably still smarting under the remarks of Goethe's previous letter, in addition to being wrought up by the coolness of the public, gave vent to his outraged feelings in a long letter to Bertuch. "Ich versichere Ihnen heilig, hätt' ich Herdern und Goethen von der Seite gekannt, als ich sie jetzt kenne, sie hätten mich nicht so glücklich machen sollen, ihre Werke zu verlegen. Sind denn 2,000 Thlr. ein Kinderspiel?"[38]

When Göschen informed Goethe that he was planning to reset the first four volumes and republish them, Goethe assumed that this was the edition in large octavo which was stipulated in the contract and expected to receive his forty complimentary copies of this edition. Bertuch, who saw Goethe's letter of October 27 before Göschen did,[39] forwarded it to Leipzig with a covering letter, and tried to reassure his partner that Goethe's biting remarks about the print and paper were nothing to worry about.

Göschen's reaction has already been noted, and he wasted no time composing a letter for Bertuch to forward to Goethe. If anything, he was now even more angry than before, as his

22

remarks to Bertuch show: "Hier ist der Brief an Goethe. Diesen muss Herder und Seidel nicht lesen. Lassen Sie ihn direct nach Rom gehen. Ich muss diese Satisfaktion an Herdern haben und alle Pfaffen hole der Teufel. . . . Noch glaub ich, Goethe wird geleitet. Sollte es nicht sein, so veracht ich ihn ebensosehr, als ich ihn verehrt habe und ich muss glauben, dass er zu den niedrigen Menschen gehört, welche glauben, alle Buchhändler sind Juden."[40] We do not know exactly what Göschen wrote to Goethe, but he must have been sufficiently tactful for Goethe to be somewhat appeased, because the answer, written on February 9, 1788, was most polite, if a trifle condescending.

Meanwhile, Göschen had not been idle. Casting around for some way of arousing public interest, he had hit upon the idea of publishing some of the works separately. Whether he ever printed as many individual copies as he had planned is not known, but bibliographers are inclined to feel that he did not, claiming that these volumes would not be so rare if Göschen had carried out his intentions. Deneke doubts whether many of the fifteen separately printed works were issued in editions of more than 1,000,[41] and we reproduce here a table compiled by Viscount Goschen to show the relatively small sale of the first eleven separate printings:

	Copies
Werther's Leiden	262
Götz von Berlichingen	20
Clavigo	17
Iphigenia	312
The Fellow-Culprits	326
Brother and Sister	292
The Triumph of Sensibility	250
The Birds	190
(Belonging to the first four volumes)	
Claudine	116
Erwin	125
Egmont	377
(Belonging to the fifth volume)[42]	

The above table is for the year 1789.

Although, as we have seen, Goethe appeared to be more kindly disposed towards Göschen after the latter had extended his apologies, this does not mean that he was prepared to change his business methods in the least. He still insisted in a letter to Seidel dated February 9, 1788, upon immediate payment of cash for any manuscript which Seidel delivered to Göschen.

Up to April 1788 the first five of the projected eight volumes had been published. Between that date and June 1789 only one more volume, the eighth, made its appearance. Despite Goethe's return to Weimar, publication could not be speeded up.

On June 22 Goethe sent to Leipzig the first pages of *Tasso*, voicing his pride that it had taken him only one year more than he had anticipated. Again he dallied, but in August he still felt Göschen would be able to publish the sixth volume in the fall. This was unfortunately not the case, since Göschen turned the tables by his delaying tactics. He was occupied with another venture, the *Historischer Kalender für Damen*, and he proposed to let Goethe cool his heels for a while.[43] Whether this was ethical is difficult to say, but he was always inclined to be a trifle hotheaded, and one must admit besides that Goethe had not set him a very good example. Besides, Göschen felt that the *Kalender* would be profitable, and he was right. It sold 6,000 copies, while Goethe's works, and *Tasso* in particular, were gathering dust on the shelves. Finally, after Goethe had expressed his displeasure to more than one person over Göschen's delay, volume six appeared in January 1790. From the tone in which Goethe wrote in these early months of 1790, he was obviously most annoyed with his publisher. One can imagine his feelings at having to wait for *Tasso*, on which he had labored for so long, while Göschen was merrily printing a *Kalender für Damen*. And so, when he eventually received his copies of volume six in late February, he wrote Göschen on March 3 a sharp letter about the illustrations and warned him to be more careful in the future.

The last volume was published in May. Writing to Knebel

24

on July 9 Goethe spoke of the editing of his work as being as laborious as it was out of the ordinary. That it had been a tiring and troublesome task for him we cannot doubt, but he had brought much of the difficulty upon himself unnecessarily.

The completion of the edition was by no means the end of the story. In April of 1791, Göschen received a long letter from Bertuch which must have disturbed him. Bertuch informed him that he had learned that Schmieder in Karlsruhe, a notorious pirate, was planning a cheap copy of Goethe's works, based directly on the authorized edition. Now in 1787 there had been some discussion between Göschen and Bertuch about preparing a separate edition in four volumes, cheap, and without the publisher's name, holding it in readiness for just such an emergency as this. This is what Göschen must have meant when he spoke of a cheap edition. The chances are that he never mentioned it to Goethe; we remember his saying that he would not mention it until the time was ripe. The first two volumes were printed in 1787 and held in abeyance. The last two were published in 1791, when the danger of piracy seemed imminent and all four were then thrown on the market. Göschen, however, had his name and the date on the title-page, so that one cannot accuse him of secretly pirating his own publication.

Both the *Goethe Jahrbuch* in 1881 and Viscount Goschen in 1903 claim that Schmieder published a pirated edition. This is apparently not the case. Deneke makes the following statement: "... es gibt überhaupt keinen Nachdruck der acht Bände der Schriften aus den Jahren 1787-1800. Insbesondere Schmieder in Karlsruhe, an den Göschen wohl besonders dachte, hat die Schriften nicht nachgedruckt." Schmieder had begun an edition in 1787, but this was a reprint of his pirated edition of Himburg's pirated edition.[44]

Following the publication of the last volume of his collected works, Goethe offered Göschen *Die Metamorphose der Pflanzen*. Göschen refused it for two reasons, although as far as we know, he divulged neither of them to Goethe. First of all, remembering all the difficulties of the past four years, he shied away from the possibility of a repetition. Secondly, he was not at all sure that he could make a profit on a scientific work by a man with no reputation in that field. He apparently went so far as to consult a botanist,[45] who assured him that Goethe's theories would never be accepted, and then he informed Goethe that he regretted that he was unable to publish the little work.

This was a mistake on Göschen's part. Had he accepted Goethe's offer, he would in all probability have been in a position to remain his publisher. By his refusal, he closed the door on the golden opportunity of publishing *Hermann und Dorothea,* which would have given him not only an enormous reputation but an enormous profit besides. Goethe received that refusal surprisingly well, and on July 4, 1791, wrote as proper a letter to Göschen as he had ever written to him. He said in part: "Es that mir leid dass Sie den kleinen Versuch der Metamorphose ausschlugen und ich war genötigt mich nach einem andern Verleger umzusehen und Verbindungen einzugehen die ich sogleich nicht lösen kann. . . . Ich kann Ihnen aufrichtig versichern dass ich sehr gewünscht hätte alles in Einer Hand zu sehen. . . . Da, wie Sie selbst sagen, meine Sachen nicht so current sind als andere an denen ein grösser Publikum Geschmack findet, so muss ich denn freylich nach den Umständen zu Werke gehen und sehe leider voraus dass sich der Verlag meiner künftigen Schriften gänzlich zerstreuen wird."[46] Many years later, when writing about this incident, Goethe realized that Göschen had some basis for his attitude, saying that it was unfortunate that the edition appeared at a time when Germany no longer knew of him and did not want to know about him.[47] But he was still somewhat surprised; he said that he could not quite understand Göschen's rejection, because by sacrificing only six sheets of paper he could have retained "einen fruchtbaren, frisch wieder auftretenden, zuverlässigen, genügsamen Autor."

If one blames Göschen for his shortsightedness on this occasion, when, as Goethe said, he stood to lose very little, one must also remember that he had had some rather harsh treatment at Goethe's hands. In addition, as we shall see, it is doubtful whether Goethe deserves his own description of himself as "einen genügsamen Autor." He was a difficult man to please, as later publishers had every opportunity to discover. But his was still a great name in German letters, even though the public had shown little enthusiasm about his recent works, and Göschen must have realized this.

What he may not have realized was that his rejection of *Die Metamorphose der Pflanzen* opened a breach between him and Goethe which was never to be permanently closed. No doubt, as time passed, and their correspondence lapsed, he began to sense that he had not done the right thing, but he was still anxious to publish for Goethe—as long as the material was of a literary rather than a scientific nature. He must have felt that Goethe was moving away from him when Unger began to publish the *Neue Schriften,* and it was perhaps this that made him put out feelers for *Hermann und Dorothea.* On April 5, 1787, Göschen told Böttiger that he would like to publish *Hermann und Dorothea* to prove to the public that Goethe had not permanently severed connections with him. However, finances would not permit this until the following Easter.[48]

These remarks show neither great enthusiasm nor enterprise on Göschen's part. If he had been anxious to show Goethe that he really wished to publish more of his work, he would have devised some means of procuring the funds necessary for such an undertaking. Any further aspirations that Göschen may have entertained of publishing later editions of Goethe's work were doomed after Goethe's visit to Cotta in 1797.

Until October 8, 1803, we hear no more from Göschen, nor is there any correspondence on Goethe's side. On that date, Göschen wrote indignantly to Böttiger, saying: "Wie ich höre, so gibt Cotta nun auch Goethes Werke heraus, ohngeachtet ich mit Goethe für die folgenden Auflagen einen bindenden Contract habe. Das ist ein feiner Bursche unter dem Mantel des Goethe-Bonaparte. Bald wird Cotta nichts mehr an *mich* zu plündern finden. Wohl möge es ihm bekommen."[49] It is quite true that Goethe was bound by contract to Göschen, after a fashion. But it is equally true that nothing was said in the contract about Goethe's being bound to offer Göschen the next *complete edition.* Section 10 of the contract stated that Goethe would offer Göschen his following works. This Goethe could have interpreted to mean any work, such as *Die Metamorphose der Pflanzen,* and following its rejection he may have felt free to change publishers. Göschen would have had a difficult time had he taken the matter to court. Of course, much of Göschen's bitterness was due to Cotta's outmaneuvering him and he resented it.

Goethe's relations with Göschen were renewed for a brief period in 1805, when Schiller, acting as intermediary, arranged to have Göschen publish *Rameaus Neffe.* This was the last contact between the two men, although they mentioned one another occasionally in later correspondence.

Göschen's opinion of Goethe seemed never to change very greatly after his angry letter to Böttiger in 1803, in spite of their temporary reassociation two years later. On the other hand, time seemed to mellow Goethe's early opinion of Göschen, and in writing the story of the publication of *Die Metamorphose der Pflanzen* he said that he had every reason to be satisfied with the publishing which Göschen had done for him.[50] This is a far cry from the letters from Italy! Again on February 14, 1821, when Goethe wrote to Knebel about the latter's translation of Lucretius, which Göschen had published, he said: "Herrn Göschen will ich den schönsten Dank sagen, dass er sich hierin, wie in so manchen andern, bereitwillig erwiesen unsere Muse zu begünstigen."

With the story of Goethe's dealing with Göschen before us in some detail, let us now see what particular problems arose out of this relationship, and how they may be explained, if explanations are possible. At this point in our study of Goethe and his publishers, we should avail ourselves of the opportunity of looking both backwards and forwards. We must set in array certain facts we already know to obtain a clear view of Goethe's reactions, and we can point the way towards similar facts and also to certain changes for the future.

One problem which arises at the very beginning of Goethe's negotiations with Göschen centers largely around Bertuch. Here is the first real instance of Goethe's use of an intermediary, a prototype, shall we say, of Mittler in *Die Wahlverwandtschaften*. It is quite true that Bertuch's services as mediator did not go beyond the early stages of the Goethe-Göschen association; nevertheless Goethe must have thought somehow that he could not bring himself to deal directly with Göschen until the contract had been signed. As we shall see, Goethe later obtained the services of two mediators par excellence in the persons of Schiller and Boisserée.

This pattern of mediation repeated itself again and again. First came the decision to publish, followed by the negotiations through a third person, and only after an agreement had been reached did Goethe correspond directly with the publisher and then only to a limited degree. Taken in a broad sense, the tone of this correspondence was very much the same throughout his life. An unmistakable note of sovereignty is sounded in the letters. Only in the case of Unger was it less noticeable and for that there were good reasons.

Goethe's elation over having been able to drive a hard bargain with Göschen is an indication of what we may expect to find in his dealings with his other publishers. His remarks to Charlotte von Stein, already quoted, were nothing more nor less than a statement of his conviction that publishers were individuals with whom one had to deal very cautiously. And yet his elation was to be short-lived. It is as though he had forgotten that he was bound by contract to Göschen.

When he realized that the preparation of his works for publication was not the simple task he had first imagined it to be, he began to sound again like the young Goethe, who was so often unwilling to make his writing public. One has the feeling that Goethe was ignorant of the pedestrian labors the publication of his collected works entailed. Perhaps it is a sign of immaturity, or of his not being at one with himself. He overestimated his own ability and underestimated the practical issues.

His state of mind revealed itself further in his letter to Göschen telling him of his projected journey to Italy. While we may consider the tone of the letter partly in the light of what Goethe thought of publishers, we cannot disregard the fact that he was emotionally upset. The lack of consideration for Göschen's feelings, and the very vague manner in which he announced his plans are but a part of that same distraction which led him to assume that he would have no trouble in living up to the promises which he had put in writing. On the other hand, his demand, in that same letter, that he be paid as the manuscript was delivered can be attributed to a practical need of money. Here he was very much the hard-headed, distrustful Goethe, who felt that publishers were rather beneath his dignity.

Goethe's irritation at having the pleasure of his experience in Italy interrupted by the ever-recurring thought that he had to complete his fragments was soon made evident. He began to feel that his whole undertaking had turned into mental torture rather than a task which he wanted to finish. And, avoiding the clear issue that he was suffering the consequences of his lack of foresight, he shifted the blame and began to vent his annoyance on Göschen: this in spite of the fact that he had definitely asserted that his work would be furthered by binding himself to a publisher. During his sojourn in Italy he did apply himself conscientiously at times, but he found it most disturbing not to be able to concentrate on his new surroundings. He was still a victim of his own inconsistency.

One assumes that Goethe realized that the many delays in the publication of the edition were as much his fault as Göschen's, but that he simply would not admit it to an "inferior" type of person. He ruffled Göschen's temper by taunting him about misprints, and in Goethe's unsettled state of mind all of Göschen's shortcomings were magnified. Possibly Goethe meant what he said about wishing to have all of his works appear under one imprint. Perhaps the two men could have cultivated a greater forbearance, but Göschen could hardly have accomplished for Goethe what Cotta did; he was simply not the man that his fellow publisher was.

It has not been our intention here to vindicate Göschen at Goethe's expense. Göschen, in spite of many admirable qualities, was too impulsive and hot-headed, and one cannot deny that at one point, at least, his business ethics could be questioned.[51] He did, however, at the beginning, lean over backwards to accommodate Goethe, protecting himself with a specific contract, but Goethe's flight to Italy left him in an awkward position. One is forced to the conclusion that this association served only to entrench more firmly Goethe's harsh opinion of the publishing guild.

Despite the publication in these years of a major body of work, one may not yet claim that Goethe had arrived at a fixed policy of wishing to see his work in print. We should remember that the initiative here was taken by Göschen and Bertuch, and also that Goethe needed money for his sojourn in Italy. A half-hearted desire to frustrate pirating may also be taken into consideration.

Other poems of the period up to 1794 furnish little indication of Goethe's feelings toward publication. He was too much taken up with larger projects to be able to pay attention to what became of these lyrics. The paucity of information from Goethe himself may indicate a lack of interest on his part. One of these poems, however, is the first example of a number of occasional poems which appeared in increasing frequency over a period of years, separately and in periodicals. The occasional poems, which for the most part are not to be counted among his best efforts, are significant in that, taken as a whole, they show a marked change in Goethe's attitude toward publication. As far as can be established, he raised no objections to their printing, and frequently seemed almost anxious that they be brought before the public. Up until about

1815 he rarely refused a request to write in honor of someone or something.

The same is true of his "Maskenzüge" and "Vorspiele," which are all part of his occasional poetry. Goethe had reason to be grateful for the treatment he had received in Weimar. He realized, no doubt, that he was no ordinary man, but was aware at the same time that his patrons had been good to him and his family. Hence his remark to P. C. Bröndsted, during the preparations for one of these "Maskenzüge": "Ja nun, man bestrebt sich, wie billig, den hohen Herrschaften als wie zum geringen Ersatz für alle Gnade und Güte zu irgendeinem gefälligen Genuss zu verhelfen."[52]

Goethe could, after all, be extremely practical, and one can assume that there was a certain amount of hard common sense in him which would tell him that the politic thing to do would be to write a poem calculated to improve his standing in the eyes of his benefactors. One does not make unflattering remarks about those upon whom one is largely dependent. Nor could anyone hold this against him, particularly when occasional poems were the order of the day. Goethe received, so far as we know, no direct financial remuneration for such poems, except in his youth, but that was not what he wanted or expected. And it is doubtful whether he thought at the time of writing that many of these poems would enhance his literary reputation among the reading public. They circulated among a relatively small and select group or were read aloud at the occasion for which they were written. In his own circle his stature as a poet might have increased, but there he was already firmly established and needed no further fame. Later on, when the time came for the publication of his works by Cotta in 1815, he thought some of these poems important enough to put them in the second volume under a separate heading: "An Personen," but this was their first appearance as a group before the general reading public.[53]

In 1791 Goethe published twenty-three epigrams, one elegy, and a prologue in *Deutsche Monatsschrift,* edited by Karl Philip Moritz and published in Berlin by Vieweg. There are two points of importance and interest concerning these poems. The first is that Goethe may have asked for payment for them, one of the few occasions when he actually was paid for a poem. He wrote to Bertuch on April 27, 1793: "Herrn Vieweg dem Älteren sendete ich meist durch Herrn Hofr. Moriz einige poetische Aufsätze. . . . Ich erinnere mich dass von 4 *Louis d'or* Honorarium fur den Bogen die Rede war. . . . Wollten Sie die Güte haben mit Herrn Vieweg die Sache abzumachen und das mir etwa zukommende Geld an sich zu nehmen. . . ." The second point in connection with this is that practically all of these epigrams appeared in print again in Schiller's *Musen-Almanach* in 1796. In other words, there seems to have been nothing to prevent an author's republishing the material he had sold to another periodical at any time that he felt so inclined. There is no evidence that he ever communicated with Vieweg about it, nor did he mention it to Schiller. And, incidentally, Goethe was paid again for these previously printed pieces, as we learn from Schiller's letter of December 8, 1795.

This episode rather suggests that from this time on Goethe was anxious to publish his individual poems. He offered Moritz the 13th elegy—apparently he took the initiative here rather than wait for someone to approach him with a request for a contribution. When Moritz accepted it, Goethe probably felt encouraged and made arrangements for all twenty-five to appear. Among those which eventually appeared was No. 256, in which he intimated that the *Deutsche Monatsschrift* was mediocre. It is curious that Goethe should disparage, in an epigram, the periodical in which his epigrams were first published, but Vieweg and Moritz apparently did not take offense, and a year later Vieweg paid Goethe a substantial sum for the manuscript of *Hermann und Dorothea,* sight unseen.

From 1791 until his association with Schiller on the *Horen,* Goethe wrote and published very little poetry indeed. But in 1794 one may claim with a fair degree of certainty that he adopted a new policy with regard to the publication of his works, particularly his poems. From now on we see him anxious to publish everything he wrote, provided he felt that it was worth while and appropriate. This is clear from his decision to publish the *Römische Elegien* and the *Venetianische Epigramme,* although he wished them to appear anonymously. In later years he did not hesitate to publish poems on scientific subjects in his *Wissenschaftliche Schriften,* and he literally forced several poems into *Wilhelm Meisters Wanderjahre* in 1821, simply to get them into print.[54] His own periodical, *Über Kunst und Altertum,* became a kind of "catch-all" for a great many poems which he wished to preserve in some kind of permanent form. At the same time, however, he was also becoming more and more particular as to what he should publish, so as not to harm his reputation. When, for instance, he was approached for a contribution by Gubitz in 1816 he hesitated, because, he said, he had seen how older men, like Gleim and Wieland, injured their reputations, the former by publishing insignificant items in insignificant journals, the latter by keeping his name on the masthead of *Merkur,* although he no longer had any connection with it.

Until about 1816, the date of the publication of the second Cotta edition of the collected works, he was convinced that he had something to offer the public, something which would be of value to them. From 1816 on, he began to feel that he might not have many more years to live. This made him all the more anxious to have his works preserved in a relatively stable and permanent state; in other words, he wished to see them printed, not to have them scattered about in manuscript form.

Chapter 2

If, as we have indicated, the year 1791 marks the beginning, however vague it may be, of a change in Goethe's attitude toward publication, then his association with Unger is a part of that change. As we shall show, the lack of a binding contract may have had its effect here. In addition, before his association with Unger came to an end, Goethe's friendship with Schiller, the success of *Hermann und Dorothea,* and his introduction to Cotta mark a period in which his publishing activities began to move rapidly forward. At the same time, while these years show a crystallization of Goethe's thinking about the appearance of his works, his behavior toward the publishers remained substantially the same.

Johann Friedrich Unger was born in Berlin in 1753. If we assume that he first came into contact with Goethe in the latter part of 1788, he was thirty-five years old when Goethe was thirty-nine. This slight difference in age would hardly account for the deferential tone of Unger's letters to Goethe, a tone which was very different from that of Göschen, and unlike Cotta, who was to succeed him as Goethe's publisher. Unger was brought up in the publishing tradition, following in his father's footsteps, and in 1780 opened his own publishing house. He was an educated man, had married the daughter of a Prussian general, and counted among his best friends such men as Zelter, Moritz, and Reichardt. Other publishers apparently thought well of him. Göschen, who referred Böttiger to him when the latter was looking for a publisher, said: "Er ist reich, hat keine Kinder und arbeitet gern um die Ehre."[1] He was something of an experimenter and artist, as his lifelong interest in woodcuts and his invention of a new and most successful type show. Gubitz, who was to become one of the most famous German artists of the woodcut, was one of his pupils.

Unger apparently went through life determined to make friends with everyone, and this may explain why he got

along so well with Goethe. There was no clash of tempera-
ment between the two. Unlike Göschen, Unger had been in
business for himself some eight years before he began to publish for Goethe, so that he may not have needed the prestige
as much as his Leipzig colleague, but there can be no doubt
that his association with Goethe helped him immensely. We
are told that only after he had published for Goethe did other
important authors turn to him.[2]

Unfortunately, with one exception, the letters of Karl
Philipp Moritz to Goethe, for whom he acted as intermediary
with Unger, have been lost, so that we have no record of how
Moritz managed to arrange with Goethe and Unger for the
publication of the *Neue Schriften*. But we do have a letter
from Unger to Goethe, written between January 5-17, 1793,
which gives us reasonable evidence that Moritz was the mid-
dleman at the beginning of the Unger-Goethe association, and
that Unger had taken the initiative in approaching Goethe.

When reading those letters from Unger to Goethe which
have been preserved, we are struck by the polite tone. In contrast to Göschen, who at times was downright rude, and even
in contrast to Cotta, who was usually more formal and businesslike, Unger was respectful almost to the point of servility.
If one can believe all that he said in his letters—and there appears to be no valid reason why one should not—he idolized
Goethe. Some may say that he was merely flattering him, as
perhaps he was, but there is often a note of sincerity which
would seem to preclude fawning. There is no doubt that
Goethe liked praise, as is evident in many of the letters in
which he mentions favorable reviews of his work, but one
doubts whether Unger realized that and capitalized on it.

Goethe's replies to Unger, which are relatively few, are
couched for the most part in polite terms, naturally with none
of the enthusiasm which the publisher shows. But judging
from the tone of his letters, he felt more at ease with Unger
than with the others. There was none of the overt friction
which characterized the negotiations with Göschen, and
Goethe must have been thankful for that.

Johann Friedrich, Freiherr von Cotta. Lithograph by
unknown artist. Courtesy of Freifrl. Blanca von Cotta
and the Deutsche Schillergesellschaft.

Johann Wolfgang Goethe. Chalk drawing by Ludwig Sebbers, 1826.

On the other hand, one cannot say that Goethe was on more intimate terms with Unger than with Göschen or Cotta. He met Unger only once (Göschen he had never met), in Leipzig in 1800, eleven years after he first began working with him. And although Unger's first publication of a work by Goethe, *Das Römische Carneval,* appeared in 1789, it is not until May 18, 1795, that we find a letter to him from Goethe. Unger had written quite frequently, but we must assume that some of Goethe's letters have been lost. In spite of the lack of correspondence, the whole relationship, which lasted until Unger's death in 1804, was a fairly friendly one, despite Goethe's condescending attitude. Only one incident, to be discussed later, marred this relationship.

Goethe's inhibition about writing directly to publishers is very much in evidence at the start of his relationship with Unger, and may account in part for the lack of correspondence in the years 1789-1794. The first notice we have of Unger's activity is a letter from the publisher to Bertuch of March 28, 1789, sending the latter the first sheets of the *Carneval.* He speaks of an edition of *Iphigenie* of 150 copies which he was printing, and which Carl August apparently had commissioned as a surprise for Goethe. Unger was evidently concerned about Göschen's reaction, since the latter held the rights to the play, and was unhappy over the fact that word of this edition had leaked to Goethe.[3]

Goethe's reaction to the first proofs of the *Carneval* is difficult to understand. On April 6, 1789, he told Carl August that the proofs were very nicely printed, but he thought the letters were too large. Then on June 29, when the whole book was in his hands, he sent a copy to Reichardt, saying: "Hier folgt der Karneval, über dessen Druck ich höchst missvergnügt bin. Ich habe diese kleine Schrift mit der grössten Sorgfalt gearbeitet und ein sehr schön geschriebnes Exemplar zum Druck gesandt, nun sind die abscheulichsten Druckfehler in den paar Bogen, die ich gar nicht mehr ansehn mag. Herr Unger sollte den Eulenspiegel auf Löschpapier drucken und sich nicht anmassen, schöne Lettern und schön Papier zu

37

missbrauchen."[4] We hear echoes of Goethe's remarks to Göschen in this letter. He was irritated when he wrote to Unger and simply let his feelings run away with him. The paper was the best obtainable at the time, and would hold its own with many modern products. Goethe's outburst over the typographical errors gives one the impression that he was simply looking for something with which he could be dissatisfied. There are not many misprints—the total is something under twenty—and only one of them can in any way be regarded as confusing to the reader. The first edition of the *Carneval* is actually an excellent piece of work.

There may be two reasons why Goethe nevertheless decided to continue with Unger as his publisher. His displeasure with Göschen undoubtedly worked to Unger's advantage, and he may have gradually forgotten his dissatisfaction with the *Carneval*. Then, too, Unger was paying him rather well. Wilhelm von Humboldt told Schiller in August of 1795 that Goethe was receiving 100 louis d'or for each volume of his *Neue Schriften*.[5] Ten days later he wrote again to Schiller, saying that according to later reports Goethe was indeed receiving 500 taler (the equivalent of 100 louis d'or) for the first four volumes, but more for *Wilhelm Meister*. The story was going the rounds that Goethe was to have 1,500 taler for the first two volumes of the novel. Humboldt continued: "Von seinem Benehmen mit seinen Verlegern, das hier durchaus hart und unbillig genannt wird, höre ich sehr viel sprechen. Indess sind auch die Berliner Gelehrten über diesen Punkt in einer ganz eigenen wahren, oder affectierten Unschuld. So fragte mich Herz neulich im ganzen Ernst, ob denn Goethe in der Tat Geld nehme?"[6]

There was no formal contract between Goethe and Unger for the publication of Goethe's *Neue Schriften*. In fact, we hear nothing about the new edition until June 26, 1792, when Goethe wrote to Georg Forster, sending him the second part of his treatise on optics. There may be a good reason for the lack of a contract here. It seems from the letter to Forster, and from other letters later on, that this whole publishing venture was not intended by Goethe as a regular edition of his works. Göschen had bound Goethe by a formal contract, containing a list of what was to be published, and had used the document as a form of advertisement. Unger either did not or could not follow this procedure, for Goethe apparently did not wish to enter into any such arrangement. There was a peculiar laxity about the entire affair; a new agreement seems to have been made for each volume or group of volumes.

The first letter we have directly from Unger to Goethe, December 15, 1792, refers only to the second volume of the *Neue Schriften*. Goethe must have been reasonably well satisfied with the first volume and considered a tentative publication of the second for Easter of 1793. He must also have mentioned *Wilhelm Meister* to Unger, since the latter asked if he might still count on publishing it when it was completed.

Unger was due for a disappointment in January, 1793, when he heard that Goethe's second volume was not to be ready by Easter. Goethe had offered him, perhaps as a sop, the last part of his *Optische Beyträge*. Unger turned down the offer, saying that since Bertuch's firm had already published the first two parts, it was too risky for another house to take over the third. He then very politely again requested Goethe to allow him to publish *Wilhelm Meister*. This little incident shows an amazing naïveté on the part of Goethe toward the business world, and points once more to the casual manner of the publication of the *Neue Schriften*.

He must have been anxious to have something of his appear soon, probably in order not to disappoint the public, which was waiting for the second volume, and in May he sent Unger the manuscript of *Der Bürgergeneral*, which the publisher acknowledged with exclamations of delight. Again we see that, since Unger was so happy to have the play and since Goethe could casually send it to replace the second volume, there can hardly be any mention of an edition of collected works. Moreover, the eventual appearance of *Reineke Fuchs*, described below, adds weight to the contention that the entire *Neue Schriften* was simply a series of separate volumes, appearing whenever author and publisher were ready, and numbered from one to seven. *Der Bürgergeneral* was not incorporated in the *Neue Schriften,* but was issued out of the series.

Goethe then wrote to Unger what must have been a long letter, promising the publisher a play[7] and *Reineke Fuchs*; the latter Unger thought would do nicely for the second volume. Unger also suggested that it be published separately in the form of an "Almanach" with illustrations by Chodowiecki, but he left the decision to the author. With the letter he sent a sample of his new type, the first of his three attempts to create a new typeface, resulting finally in the now famous "Unger-Fraktur." He suggested that if Goethe liked it, he could use it for the remaining volumes.

Goethe was most gracious about the publication of *Reineke Fuchs* and left it entirely in the hands of Unger, who decided, on November 30, to make it the second volume of the *Neue Schriften*. He claimed that time would not permit of an "Almanach" publication, which was probably another way of saying that Goethe had held him up long enough and that he could not afford to postpone a second volume any longer. He enclosed a second example of new type for Goethe's approval.

Goethe's procrastination must have been a source of considerable annoyance for Unger, but we should give him credit for never losing his temper. He had a way of hinting that Goethe might perhaps bestir himself a bit by phrasing his thoughts in the form of fervently polite wishes. He must at times have expressed his irritation to friends, but no doubt realized that he stood to gain by retaining his equanimity and there can be little doubt that this pleased Goethe. This is further borne out by the incident of Unger's publication in 1794 of an English translation of *Iphigenie*.[8] Goethe told Unger that he had received it, and probably suggested that he republish it. There was no question of piracy here, particularly in the case of a translation, since copyright laws between different countries did not exist. The interesting point is that Goethe wished to do Unger a favor.

In February, 1794, Unger sent Goethe the third and final sample of his newest type—that which is now "Unger-Fraktur"—and on April 15 he went into rhapsodies over the fact that Goethe had consented to his publishing *Wilhelm Meisters Lehrjahre*. "Würden Sie es wohl genehmigen, dass ich, um den Nachdruck einigermassen zu hemmen, ein *ganz einfache* Pränumerationsanzeige ins Publikum ergehen liesse? . . . Ein Buch von *Ihnen* ist viel zu verehrungswerth, als dass der Verleger sich unterstehen dürfte, die Ankündigung davon mit einem Marktschreierton zu besudeln." Included with the letter he sent a contract in which he committed himself to pay Goethe 600 taler in louis d'or for each volume of manuscript of the new novel. This would make a total of 2,400 taler for the four volumes. The signing of a contract for these volumes alone is again indicative of the haphazard manner of publication. It was as though Unger, following the appearance of each separate work, was never quite sure whether Goethe would send another.

The *Lehrjahre* forms volumes 3-6 of the *Neue Schriften* as we now have them, but before Unger could begin publication he had to get *Reineke Fuchs* off his press. Not until July did Goethe send him the first part of the manuscript of the new novel. In the meantime, Goethe was busy finding misprints in *Reineke Fuchs* and he wasted no time, as was his wont, in communicating with the publisher on the subject. Unger was devastated, but cleverly made no excuses, suggesting on June 4 that it would solve the problem if Goethe himself consented to read final proof, and saying on June 13 that it was important that publication be slowed in order to be as careful as possible.

In this same letter Unger made a request of Goethe which was to assure him success and fame, asking permission to use for the *Lehrjahre* his newly developed type. He admitted quite frankly that it would be of enormous advantage to him if the great Goethe were to be the first author to have his work printed with his "Fraktur," and, as it turned out, he was quite right. Now it is hardly conceivable that, had

Goethe looked upon the publication of the *Neue Schriften* as a complete edition, he would have consented to a change of type in the middle of the edition. He must then have regarded these four volumes as an entity which Unger might work into his series as he saw fit.[9]

Up until May 1795, everything went smoothly with *Wilhelm Meister*; on the 7th of that month Unger could write hoping that Goethe had received the completed second volume. At the same time he expressed a wish that Goethe, since he was planning another journey to Italy, write of his experiences on the trip and send the account to Unger for publication. This wish was never fulfilled.[10] Shortly before this, Goethe had apparently offered Unger another projected work for publication: *Beobachtungen und Betrachtungen über Gegenstände aus der Naturgeschichte und Naturlehre,* which Unger gratefully accepted. This was a plan which Goethe never carried out; in fact, the work was never written, but arrangements were made for a volume in large octavo with illustrations. Unger was now beginning to see results from his new type, and we quote here from a letter of May 23 to illustrate his general attitude towards Goethe in the correspondence: "Ihnen, verehrungswürdigster Mann, verdanke ich das Glück, das itzt die neuen deutschen Buchstaben beim Publikum machen, da Sie solche mit Ihrem Beifall beehrten, und es erlaubten, dass ein so herrliches Produkt von Ihnen damit gedruckt werden durfte. Ohne diese Erlaubniss wäre es lange noch nicht mit dieselben [sic] dahin gekommen, sie so häufig zu gebrauchen, als man es jetzt schon thut.—Muss man nicht das Publikum schätzen, das sich nach dem Geschmack eines *Göthe* richtet?"

Between August 1795 and March 1796 Unger was repeatedly forced to write urging Goethe to send him manuscript so that he could complete the printing of *Wilhelm Meisters Lehrjahre,* and Goethe kept putting him off. At one point he offered Unger a French translation of the sixth book of the novel for publication![11] Here we have a prime example of Goethe's sovereign attitude.

Between March and September of 1796, Goethe apparently delivered manuscript fairly regularly, but not without a certain amount of tactful prodding from his publisher, and *Wilhelm Meister* was finished in October.

During the year 1796 Unger had further reason to be annoyed with Goethe, but again tactfully gave him no inkling of his feelings, airing his irritation instead to a fellow publisher, Friedrich Nicolai, who had been at odds with Goethe for a good many years. One of the *Xenien* of 1796 reads thus:

Die Eiche.
Lasset euch ja nicht zu Ungers altdeutscher Eiche verführen,
Ihre styptische Frucht nähret kein reinliches Tier.

This, according to Biedermann, was directed at the Unger-Reichardt periodical, *Deutschland,* and he claims further that the medical term *styptisch* points to Schiller as the author rather than Goethe.[12]

Possibly the silence which followed now was Unger's way of expressing his displeasure. For it was not until February 11 that he addressed himself to Goethe again, politely inquiring when he might hope to see manuscript for the 7th volume of the *Neue Schriften.* Goethe again bided his time, writing on March 3, 1797, that he had something almost ready, but that there were a few other smaller items which he felt should be brought to the notice of the public first. Now Goethe had meantime been negotiating with Vieweg behind Unger's back, but probably Unger knew something about it. Since both publishing houses were in Berlin, each had a fairly good idea of what the other was doing, and a remark of Unger's in his letter of February 11 hints at this: "Ich will mich sehr glücklich schätzen, wenn Ihnen mein bisheriges Betragen keine Veränderung des Verlegers zu veranstalten nöthigt, und warte sehnsuchtsvoll auf Ihre Antwort."

There followed then a long period of silence, when no letters traveled between Weimar and Berlin, but in October, Unger, having heard of Goethe's visit to Tübingen, where he was Cotta's guest from the 6th to the 11th of September, and hearing nothing from Goethe himself, must have become suspicious. He must also have been hoping to acquire *Faust* for publication, judging from the following remarks to Böttiger on October 10: "Wenn H. v. Goethe wieder in Weimar ist, werde ich wohl das nähere erfahren; auch werde ich von Berlin an ihn schreiben, und wenn Sie nicht wollen, des Fausts gar nicht erwähnen. Ist und kann mir mein so sehr verehrter Goethe darum abtrünnig werden, weil ein anderer Buchhändler ihn 4 Wochen bewirtet hat, nun so sage ich weiter nichts dazu." However, he seemed determined not to think ill of either of them, and continued: "Nur glaube ich, dass dies ein jeder andre, der auch kein Buchhändler gewesen wäre, mit Freuden und ohne alles andre Interesse getan haben würde, wenn so ein lieber grosser Mann hätte bei ihm einkehren wollen. Genug hiervon; ich warte die Sache geduldig ab."

Even Unger's patience gave out after another three months, but he reminded Goethe as politely as ever on January 13, 1798, that almost two years had passed since he had been privileged to print something by the great man. Goethe replied on January 30, 1798, that his trip to Switzerland had, of course, interrupted his literary activities, but that he hoped soon to be able to submit some sort of manuscript.

Unger, it seems, was not particularly disturbed by the fact that Goethe had had Vieweg publish *Hermann und Dorothea*; in fact, he must have had a long friendly conversation with Vieweg about it. He had only one minor complaint to make in a letter of February 11, that the edition was not elegant enough; and he seemed to think that, had Vieweg not kept his intentions of publishing the poem secret, his [Unger's] technical suggestions would have met with Vieweg's approval.

Goethe, who apparently now had nothing which he could offer Unger, since he was so preoccupied with the *Musen-Almanach,* found himself in an embarrassing situation. Unger did not press him, but in May 1799, tactfully reminded Goethe that the latter had previously hinted at a seventh volume of the *Neue Schriften.* Goethe answered through Schiller, who wrote to Unger on the 25th of May, telling him that he had suggested to Goethe that he collect the fugitive poems written and published in the past eight years and use them for the seventh volume.[13]

When Unger next wrote to Goethe, on the 23rd of July, he quoted Schiller almost verbatim. He also had a complaint to make about Vieweg, telling Goethe that Vieweg had published another edition of *Hermann und Dorothea,* calling it the first volume of Goethe's *Neue Schriften,* and asking whether Goethe had authorized this. Unger was naturally upset because people now thought that the *Neue Schriften* were no longer published by him.

As far as we can ascertain, this move of Vieweg's was merely a liberty which he took, one of the many examples of what any publisher could do in order to promote his sales in the absence of proper protective legislation. We have Goethe's word for it that he had given Vieweg no such authorization. Writing on August 5, 1799, he told Unger that so far he had every reason to be satisfied with Vieweg, but that he could not sanction this latest move, especially since they had never discussed the matter. There is, however, no evidence that Goethe remonstrated with Vieweg on this point, although he may have, since Unger had nothing further to say about it.

Although the Goethe-Cotta negotiations were only in the preliminary stages, plans were being made, and they do affect Goethe's association with Unger. Goethe told Cotta in confidence on September 22, 1799, that Unger would print, as volume 7, some of the fugitive poems, and perhaps something similar could be used for the eighth. Other than this, he said, he had no commitments. This sounds very much as though Goethe were saying that as soon as his obligations to Unger were fulfilled, he would be prepared to discuss business matters with Cotta.

On November 4, he sent to Unger some manuscript for volume 7 of the *Neue Schriften.* The letter accompanying it is a fine example of the detailed instructions with which Goethe used to bedevil his publishers. Each poem must be on

45

a new page. The sequence of poems must not be changed. The illustrations which Goethe sent must be reproduced accurately. There must be a vignette on the title-page. Unger must be most careful to avoid typographical errors, and so on. One sentence indicates that Goethe was thinking seriously of making this the last volume of the series, since he had tentatively committed himself to Cotta. The sentence reads: "An eine grössere Arbeit darf ich vorerst nicht denken und möchte nicht eher ein Werk zusagen als bis es auch wirklich fertig wäre." Over and above these implications, the letter shows an interesting inconsistency in Goethe's character. We have hitherto observed the haphazard manner in which he was conducting his association with Unger. Now he became definite, and laid down specific rules for the printing of a certain volume.

Unger went to work immediately. The letters in the following months show that everything proceeded according to plan and that Goethe was quite pleased with the preliminary results. Some time after April 1800, the seventh volume of the *Neue Schriften* was completed, and there was then another long pause in correspondence. In March, 1801, Unger wrote briefly to say how happy he was that Goethe had recovered from a recent illness, but made no reference to any further publication. During this period and for some time afterwards Unger was busy with Schiller, both in connection with the *Musen-Almanach* and Schiller's works. A letter to Schiller of March 14 gave him the opportunity to ask whether Goethe was planning an eighth volume. Unger was still worried, but did not dare approach Goethe directly for fear of antagonizing him. It is not clear whether Schiller spoke to his friend about it, but in any case Goethe took no action, for on May 19, 1802, Unger mentioned the subject again. Goethe did not even bother to answer, whereupon Unger wrote once more after a year had passed, saying reproachfully that he could not understand why Goethe was punishing him by keeping silent.[14]

Goethe's conscience finally got the better of him, and he replied on June 8, 1803, thanking Unger, but still saying nothing at all about further publication. On July 10, Unger wrote again very graciously, acknowledging Goethe's letter and asking if it would not be possible to publish *Die natür- liche Tochter,* along with anything else Goethe had at hand, as the eighth volume of the *Neue Schriften.* Goethe was really embarrassed now, since on May 15, 1803, he had for- mally contracted to have several works published by Cotta, including *Die natürliche Tochter.* He wrote a rather naïve letter to Zelter about it on August 29, saying: "Herr Unger schreibt mir vor einiger Zeit um einen achten Theil. Ich kann weder zu- noch absagen. Nicht ab, weil ich wirklich gern die Zahl voll machte, nicht zu, weil meine nächsten Arbeiten an Cotta versagt sind, mit dem ich sehr zufrieden zu seyn Ursache habe. Mögen Sie Herrn Unger ein freundliches Wort darüber sagen, dass er mein Stillschweigen nicht un- gleich auslege."[15] Goethe apparently did not find it con- venient to tell Unger what the truth was, but had to have a friend try to smooth the matter over. Even taking into ac- count Goethe's dislike of direct correspondence with a pub- lisher, one would think that he would address his remarks directly to Unger in such a situation. Perhaps stranger than Goethe's assumption that Unger would be soothed by a few tactful remarks from Zelter is the fact that this was presum- ably what actually happened, because there was no further correspondence between the two men. Unger died on De- cember 26, 1804.[16]

One cannot help having the feeling that Unger's death was, for Goethe, quite convenient. How he felt about it we shall probably never know, for he apparently did not take the time to say, nor did he, as far as we know, write to Frau Unger to extend condolences, but we would not be surprised if he did not perhaps feel rather relieved. With Unger's death, the pressure from Berlin was removed, and the Goethe- Cotta relationship now rested on a much firmer foundation.

The whole relationship between Goethe and Unger gives the impression that Goethe thought of Unger as a lower type of individual—perhaps for no other reason than that he was a publisher. We should remember that his distrust and dislike of publishers was a state of mind which could not be permanently altered under any circumstances, no matter how favorable the relationship.

All in all, from Goethe's point of view the relationship with Unger was as satisfactory as any he enjoyed with his publishers, largely because Unger did as Goethe wished him to. If he was displeased with his work, as in the case of the printing of the *Römisches Carneval,* he wrote no unpleasant letters directly to Unger as he did to Göschen. Unger likewise, as far as we can ascertain, kept any resentment he may have had towards Goethe a secret from him. He obviously admired him, even though Goethe was a sore trial to his patience and often unfair. Once Goethe had recovered from his anger at the *Carneval* he was reasonably well disposed towards Unger—in a patronizing sort of way, to be sure—nevertheless well disposed. It was not until he became acquainted with Cotta, and began to realize that greater advantages lay in that direction, that the tie with Unger, weak as it was, developed into a source of annoyance to him.

II

The story of Goethe's relationship to Friedrich Vieweg of Berlin is to all intents and purposes the story of the publication of *Hermann und Dorothea.* We know that in 1790 Goethe published a few epigrams in Vieweg's *Deutsche Monatsschrift,* but the records give no indication of any personal or written contact between author and publisher at that time.

We have seen how Goethe broke with Göschen following the latter's refusal to publish the *Metamorphose der Pflanzen,* and how Böttiger apparently broached the subject of *Hermann und Dorothea* to Göschen in 1795. Göschen hesitated because of financial worries and the memory of previous experiences, so that Goethe accepted Böttiger's recommendations for a new publisher.

Böttiger, since the middle of November 1796, had been

corresponding with Vieweg on the subject of a *Taschenbuch,* which Vieweg wished to devote to a work of Goethe. Toward the end of November Böttiger laid Vieweg's plan before Goethe, along with proofs of a few pages of the proposed volume.[17] (Apparently then, the initiative was Vieweg's rather than either Goethe's or Böttiger's.) Goethe agreed to the proposition, and on January 16, 1797, wrote the following letter to Vieweg:

Ich bin geneigt Herrn Vieweg in Berlin ein episches Gedicht *Hermann und Dorothea* das ohngefähr 2000 Hexameter stark seyn wird zum Verlag zu überlassen. Und zwar dergestalt dass solches den Inhalt seines Almanachs auf 1798 ausmache und dass ich nach Verlauf von 2 Jahren allenfalls dasselbe in meinen Schriften wieder aufführen könne. Was das Honorar betrifft so stelle ich Herrn Oberconsistorialrath Böttiger ein versiegeltes Billet zu, worin meine Forderung enthalten ist und erwarte was Herr Vieweg mir für meine Arbeit anbieten zu können glaubt. Ist sein Anerbieten geringer als meine Forderung, so nehme ich meinen versiegelten Zettel uneröffnet zurück, und die Negotiation zerschlägt sich, ist es höher, so verlange ich nicht mehr als in dem, alsdann von Herrn Oberconsistorialrath zu eröffnenden Zettel verzeichnet ist.

To Böttiger he wrote on the same day: "Für das episches Gedicht *Hermann und Dorothea* verlange ich Eintausend Thaler in Golde," and on the cover of this note: "Herr Oberconsistorialrath Böttiger wird ersucht gegenwärtiges bis zur bekannten Epoche bey sich uneröffnet liegen zu lassen."

Even stranger than Goethe's method of negotiation with Vieweg is the fact that the latter, as we can see from Goethe's answer to him on January 30, offered exactly 1,000 taler. Three explanations of this have been advanced: first, that the envelope containing Goethe's demand was transparent;[18] second, that somehow or other Böttiger knew what Goethe was asking and told Vieweg;[19] third, that this note was never actually written, but was erroneously reconstructed from the files of the Vieweg publishing house.[20]

No one is willing to suggest that it could be mere coincidence, owing to the fact that the sum was regarded by contemporaries as an extraordinarily large one. Caroline von Humboldt thought so, and she tells us Schiller agreed with her. She gives us an interesting piece of information as to Goethe's feelings on the matter, saying that Schiller told her that he had asked Goethe whether he was satisfied with the honorarium, and the answer was: "O ja, recht gut, ich kann leidlich zufrieden sein." Goethe saw nothing out of the ordinary in it.[21]

Apparently the "Calenderform" appealed to Goethe for two reasons, since he told Meyer on March 18 that in this format the poem would have the widest circulation and would bring the largest remuneration. The *Taschenbuch für 1798,* in which the poem appeared, would naturally have a larger circulation than a volume appended to the *Neue Schriften.* There is, however, no record of Unger ever being approached on this subject.

In Goethe's answer to Vieweg acknowledging receipt of the publisher's offer, he was very careful to emphasize the fact that Vieweg should have the rights only for two years following publication. We shall see later that Vieweg had no scruples about disregarding this stipulation.

A point to be made here is that in spite of Goethe's not infrequent criticisms of periodicals, he nevertheless considered the *Taschenbuch* and *Almanach* type of journal to be of the utmost importance. This is borne out by his many poetic contributions to such publications, by his remarks about the *Berliner Musen-Almanach* of 1831, and by the fact that he had one of his most famous works published in *Taschenbuch* form. Undoubtedly, as we have seen, he was influenced in the last instance by the large circulation, but it is by no means certain that he would have done the same thing for less reputable journals, even for the sake of a larger circulation.

In June or July of 1798, Vieweg must have written to Goethe suggesting that he issue a second edition and also requesting an extension of the publication rights. Goethe's indecision and his unwillingness to grant this extension led to difficulties. On July 12, he wrote to Vieweg that he was a little embarrassed because he did not quite know what to say. He would probably not plan to have a second edition published immediately, but neither did he specifically wish to extend Vieweg's publishing rights, "da so manche Umstände eintreten können unter welchen man nicht gebunden zu seyn wünscht." This might be interpreted to mean that he was already interested in Cotta as his publisher and was seriously considering a change. At any rate, he now had to contend with Vieweg's using the words "Neue Schriften" on the 1799 edition of *Hermann und Dorothea* and had to soothe Unger's feelings, although he did not appear to be particularly aroused by Vieweg's presumption.

From this point Goethe seemed to have dropped Vieweg entirely and to have lost interest in his activities, although it can hardly have escaped his notice that Vieweg issued so-called "new editions" in 1803, 1805, 1806 and 1807, and two in 1814. As a matter of fact, in January 1808 Cotta, who was obviously more perturbed about this illegal publication than Goethe, wrote to the latter asking about his present relationship with Vieweg, to which Goethe replied that Vieweg's activities were simple piracy.

In the absence of legal machinery, there was nothing that either Goethe or Cotta could do about this, but one cannot help feeling that Goethe's lack of interest in the matter must have encouraged Vieweg. Naturally the latter was in the wrong, but so far as we know, Goethe never even protested to him. It had seemed that everything was satisfactory until Vieweg, spurred on probably by Goethe's vacillation, published in defiance of the original agreement, and finding that Goethe did not object, issued one edition after another.

III

As we have seen, even while Goethe was still involved with Unger and Vieweg, he had made the acquaintance of Johann Friedrich Cotta, and had taken the first steps toward granting him publication rights.

The 37-year association between Goethe and Cotta was effected by Schiller, following Goethe's acceptance of the invitation to contribute to the *Horen,* which Cotta published. As in the case of Schiller, the relationship with Cotta proved to be of the utmost importance for the history of German letters, although one can scarcely claim that Goethe and Cotta were ever really intimate friends. They were never as close as Schiller and Cotta were, but this is hardly surprising, now that we are reasonably familiar with Goethe's attitude toward the publishing world. He unquestionably benefited more from his association with Cotta than with any of his other publishers; Cotta's generosity and his willingness to undertake what to lesser men must have appeared as very risky enterprises did have a benign effect on Goethe, but he would not or could not entirely change his opinion of publishers even after long association with a man of Cotta's stature.

Cotta was no ordinary publisher; in fact, he was altogether an extraordinary person. His activities were by no means limited to the book trade; he was a man of many enterprises, a keen mathematician, a sharp legal thinker, the proprietor of large estates, a patron of the arts, a politician whose perseverance and far-sightedness did much for his country, and a man who could just as easily have stepped into a career as a leading diplomat as that of the foremost publisher of his age. A list of the authors whose works appeared over his name will show that many of the great names in German literature from 1787 to 1836 were on it. In addition to Goethe and Schiller, we find Herder, Hölderlin, Wieland, Jean Paul, Voss, Mathisson, Schelling, Fichte, Tieck, Hebel, the brothers von Humboldt, Spittler, the Schlegels, and others. He was not only an extremely intelligent businessman who paid his authors well but also one who was genuinely interested in the arts. He gave Wieland sixty ducats for a small *Taschenbuch* which contained but two stories, in contrast to the offer by another publisher of seven taler for Wieland's *Musarion.*[22] When, in 1794, he arranged for Schiller to become editor of the *Allgemeine Zeitung,* the contract stated that he was to receive 2,000 florins regardless of circulation, and made provisions to raise the stipend with an increase in circulation.[23] And he hesitated not a moment when Schiller suggested that Goethe would expect to be well paid for his contributions to the *Horen,* but agreed that he ought to receive a substantial sum. It is natural that such generosity would make authors gravitate towards him, but we should not think that he was merely practicing bribery by offering large payments to authors whose works he felt would be profitable. Such is not the case. Cotta did not publish "penny dreadfuls" or books containing "blood and thunder," which would assuredly have had a wide circulation. On the contrary, one's impression is that he was generous because he felt that a man who had something worth while to offer deserved a commensurate return. He was the type of man who, having contracted to pay an author a set amount for a work, would pay him that amount even if it meant losing on the publication. This happened in the case of both Schiller and Goethe. In addition, Cotta rarely, if ever, refused an advance on royalties to authors with whom he was associated.

We know that Goethe tried to keep his social and business relationships apart, if humanly possible. We know, too, that Schiller was quite right when he told Cotta not to expect from Goethe better treatment than other publishers. At the beginning of the correspondence between them Goethe was very proper and correct. There was none of the brusqueness with which he sometimes addressed Göschen, and little of the condescension which one finds in letters to Unger and Vieweg. There is a reason for this: it is certain that Goethe, following his visit to Cotta in 1797, was impressed by him, probably because Cotta did not immediately fit his preconceived notion of a publisher. In all probability, we can take at face value what he wrote to Schiller on September 12 during his stay in Tübingen: "Je näher ich Herrn Cotta kennen lerne, desto besser gefällt er mir. Für einen Mann von strebender Denkart und unternehmender Handelsweise, hat er so viel mässiges, sanftes und gefasstes, so viel Klarheit und Beharrlich-keit, dass er mir eine seltne Erscheinung ist."

Just what Goethe and his host discussed during their week together is not known, but judging from the few letters which immediately follow Goethe's return it is likely that there was some conversation in guarded and indefinite terms on the possibility that Cotta might publish something which Goethe would be prepared to entrust to him. At any rate, on January 1, 1798, Goethe wrote thanking Cotta once more for his hospitality, and saying that he had collected a great deal of material on his trip. He went on to say that he thought much of his success was due to Cotta's assistance and he hoped to be able to send him something in return. We can safely assume that this "something" was of a literary nature, rather than simply a gift sent in appreciation, and Goethe may very well have had in mind a contribution to one of Cotta's periodicals, *Neueste Weltkunde,* for on January 20, Cotta, writing to Schiller, remarked: "Herr Geheimerath v. Goethe bitte ich doch auch hiezu zu vermögen, er hat mir schon grosse Hoffnungen gemacht."[24]

Relations between Goethe and Cotta were more firmly cemented by the editor-publisher partnership on the *Propyläen*. At the outset it becomes clear that Cotta had made a favorable impression on Goethe. This does not mean that Goethe left matters entirely in Cotta's hands; he still did not hesitate to inform him of typographical errors, but his letters were far more reserved than those to other publishers. He said that he would like to have certain pages of the *Propyläen* reprinted, but only if it would not inconvenience Cotta too greatly. And in a naïve, unconsciously condescending, but well-meaning way he advised Cotta on December 7, 1798, that his publications would be better received if more care were taken in the rendering of foreign words and technical ex-pressions. The number of letters in which Goethe dispensed his advice must have become a trifle wearisome for Cotta, al-though he apparently never objected, probably because he had been warned by Schiller to expect advice and criticism. Goethe was obviously not going to relax his standards, but at the same time he sensed somehow that Cotta was more than just another publisher.

Another incident which may bear out the contention that Goethe entertained a certain respect for Cotta was the failure of the *Propyläen*. When, on June 17, 1799, Cotta wrote saying that the circulation of the periodical was far below what he had anticipated, and that he would probably lose money on it, Goethe seemed little worried.[25] Particular as he was about details of typography, a larger problem did not affect him in the same way. One might imagine that he would have been inclined to blame either the publisher or the public for the failure, but he blamed nobody, and perhaps for the first time in his life he saw matters from the publisher's point of view rather than from his own. At any rate, he was extraordinarily philosophical about it, as we can see from his letter to Cotta of July 5, 1799: "Uebrigens bedarf diese Eröffnung keiner Entschuldigung da die Nothwendigkeit sie Ihnen abdringt, und mir ist dabey das erfreuliche dass ich, bey diesem unangenehmen Fall, in Ihnen den Mann gleichfalls sehe der mir eine so vorzügliche Hochachtung abgewonnen hat."

This letter could show two things: Goethe's high personal regard for Cotta, and an ability to accept failure, but it is difficult not to think of something else. Knowing as we do Goethe's attitude in financial matters, we should bear in mind what he might have been thinking: Cotta had lost 2,500 florins,[26] not he, so that it would be comparatively easy for him to adopt the "try, try again" attitude. Hence it may have been merely a gesture on his part when, on September 22, he told Cotta that naturally the publisher was not expected to assume the entire burden of financial loss, and that he would gladly accept any reduction of his payment—within reason.[27]

We know that Goethe assured Cotta that as soon as the *Neue Schriften* were out of the way he would have no obligations to any other publisher. But he went even farther than that, and possibly he felt that he should try to make up to Cotta for the financial buffeting that the publisher had taken with the *Propyläen*. He said that in all fairness he should give Cotta priority on anything else which he might finish in the near future. "Dieses war bey mir schon früher ein stiller Vorsaz," he wrote on September 22, "den mir Ihr Charackter und Ihre Handelsweise abnöthigten eh mir die letzten Ereignisse noch mehr Verbindlichkeit gegen Sie auferlegten." The only drawback to his promise was that it was not until two and a half years later that he actually had something which he could offer for publication.

In the meantime, the *Propyläen* died a natural death, without any real expressions of regret on anyone's part, although its passing brought forth some acid remarks from Schiller on the intelligence and taste of the German public. He probably felt unhappier about it than anyone else, particularly since he had done his utmost to persuade Cotta to publish the periodical.

The correspondence between Goethe and Cotta from the end of September 1799 until the end of March 1802 is very sparse, and Cotta was worried about it, as we learn from his letters to Schiller. He was anxious to have *Faust* for publication, but Goethe simply could not bring himself to finish it. On November 17, 1800, he excused himself by saying that the task of completing it was like judging distances on a journey —they were always greater than one at first imagined. Schiller threw some light on the situation, however, when he wrote on December 10, 1801, in answer to a query from Cotta as to why he had not heard from Goethe: "Er ist zu wenig Herr über seine Stimmung, seine Schwerfälligkeit macht ihn unschlussig und über den vielen LiebhaberBeschäftigungen, die er sich mit Wissenschaftlichen Dingen macht, zerstreut er sich zu sehr." This is undoubtedly a valid explanation, but is it not perhaps possible that the failure of the *Propyläen* had more of an effect on Goethe than he cared to admit? Could it be that his rejection, so to speak, by the public had discouraged him temporarily from any further publishing which he may have had in mind, and encouraged him to devote himself for a time to research in the sciences? We know that as a general rule he paid little attention to public opinion, but since one of the objects of the *Propyläen* was to try to educate the reading public away from its strange taste in literature to a higher level, the reaction may have had a part in turning him from publication. Another reason, advanced by Schiller to account for the long silence, was Goethe's annoyance over complaints that he thought Cotta had made to Böttiger about the circulation of the *Propyläen*. Whether these reasons are true in whole or only in part, the fact remains that Goethe, having assured Cotta that he was entitled to be the first to accept or reject any fresh manuscript, sailed into the literary doldrums and did not emerge until the beginning of 1802.[28]

On March 30 he wrote Cotta that he had reworked Voltaire's tragedies, *Mahomet* and *Tancred,* and in contrast to his usual practice of trying to have the publisher make him an offer, he said briefly that Cotta could have both plays for 500 taler. Cotta paid without demurring, since Goethe acknowledged the receipt of the money on May 30, and the publication of *Mahomet* marked one of the few occasions when he was really pleased with the physical appearance of one of his works when it reached him from the publisher.

Goethe's next offer to Cotta was the *Vorspiel* written for the opening of the Lauchstädt theater, and for the negotiations he relied partly upon himself, partly upon Schiller. He told Cotta that as far as payment was concerned, Schiller would settle that—after he had written to Schiller about it. Strange that only a short time before he had had no difficulty whatsoever in asking a definite price from Cotta, and now he felt on August 13 that it would be hard to name a sum. At the same time he was driving his first hard bargain with his new publisher about *Cellini,* with Schiller as intermediary.

Goethe insisted that Cotta publish it if he wanted anything else from him. Schiller had communicated with Cotta on March 28, 1798, saying: "Es fragt sich nun ob Sie Lust dazu haben, und welche Bedingungen Sie machen können, denn wohlfeil giebt es Goethe nicht." On April 11 Cotta replied not too enthusiastically, saying that he was a little worried about Goethe's terms, but that he certainly did not wish to terminate his relationship with him because of the *Cellini.* He would be quite satisfied if Schiller could influence Goethe to offer him future works, especially *Faust.* On April 27 Schiller wrote Goethe that Cotta was hesitant about *Cellini,* and he then suggested that Goethe offer Cotta his next work, perhaps *Faust,* but made the whole thing sound as though it were his own idea rather than Cotta's.

On May 18, 1802, Schiller told Cotta that Goethe wished to publish an almanac of songs the following year. He emphasized that Goethe's name and the melodies would make for a large sale and assured Cotta that he could safely pay the 1,000 taler which Goethe wanted, although he did admit that a great number of copies would have to be sold if Cotta wanted any return on his investment. He continued: "Hiebei aber ist eine Bedingung welche mir bedenklich scheint. Goethe will nehmlich, dass Sie auch zwey andere Werke, Winckelmann und sein Jahrhundert und Benvenuto Cellini, vielleicht auch mehrere, binnen der nächsten Jahre verlegen." He went on to say that these would, of course, have nothing like the sale of the songs but that Goethe remained adamant and that if Cotta wanted the latter he would have to take the other works too. The publisher met Goethe's terms, although he must have known that he was taking a risk, for even as late as March 1803, Goethe was still not sure what he was going to include in his *Taschenbuch.*

After Cotta had come to terms and *Cellini* had appeared, Goethe decided that it would be advisable to have some sort of document covering their agreement. What resulted from this decision was the first contract with Cotta, if one can call it that, since it was rather informal. It stipulated that Cotta would publish one edition each of *Was wir bringen, Benvenuto Cellini, Die natürliche Tochter,* and "eine Anzahl neuer Lieder," the last being Goethe's contribution to the *Taschenbuch auf das Jahr 1804.* At the date of signing, May 15, 1803, the first two items had already been published, a fact which in itself makes the contract somewhat unusual.

This account of some of Goethe's publishing activities gives us a glimpse of several of the characteristics which reveal themselves again and again throughout his lifetime. The mediation of a third person, the harsh demands made by the author upon the publisher, the uncertainty which existed—sometimes up until the last moment—these three in particular were familiar to all of Goethe's publishers at one time or another. As we shall see later, it was extremely difficult for Goethe to negotiate directly. He did not really trust publishers, nor did he feel that he should have to descend to their level. This feeling accounts in part for the demands he made upon them. He felt it his privilege to change his mind as often as he desired, and if he often disregarded their feelings and acted inconsiderately, that was no concern of his.

Chapter 3

The third period of Goethe's publishing activity falls between the years 1804 and 1816. This covers the first two editions of his collected writings published by Cotta and almost all of the later major works which appeared separately.

A few months after Goethe had entered into an agreement with Cotta for the publication of *Cellini*, he began to think seriously of a new edition of his works. The first intimation we have of his intentions is in a letter from Schiller to Cotta of October 16, 1804, in which Schiller was still the intermediary. Goethe wished this proposed edition to be a simple one.[1] The stipulations which he communicated to Schiller were rather harsh, at least harsh enough to make the publisher balk and suggest easier terms. Goethe wished the edition to be completed within one and a half years, the publishing rights to last five years from the date of the appearance of the first volume. In the days when mass production was unknown, these were hard terms, and Schiller could sympathize with Cotta when he said: "Der Verleger müsste sich also freilich tummeln, um in diesem kurzen Zeitraum das Werk zu verkaufen." Goethe's method of broaching the subject here is of interest, as it serves to illustrate further the inconsistency with which he handled such matters. In some cases he preferred only to mention the fact that he was thinking of publishing and then to sit back and wait. In others he would go further and ask the publisher to state his terms. Such a procedure would put him in the position of being able to accept, reject, or bargain as he saw fit. At other times, and this instance is a case in point, he changed his tactics and stated his own terms with a "take-it-or-leave-it" attitude.

Cotta, who was most anxious to have Goethe commission him to publish a major work, told Schiller on October 26 that he would gladly undertake publication under two conditions: that the time allotted for publication be extended and that he be permitted to retain the rights for either six or seven years. He had in the meantime heard from Schiller that Goethe expected to receive between 1,520 and 1,600 carolin for the manuscript, and he was prepared to pay it.[2]

From January 1, 1804, to June 14, 1805, Goethe wrote to Cotta only three times. On the date last mentioned he sent to him a memorandum declaring his intention to publish and enumerating the volumes and their contents. On December 13, 1804, Schiller had told Cotta that for a long time he had heard nothing from Goethe about the proposed edition and that the latter was apparently not giving it much consideration. We can suggest reasons why there was at this time so little correspondence. Cotta was probably much too busy arranging with Schiller for the publication of *his* collected works. Goethe may have been awaiting a visit from Cotta in order to discuss the matter in person, and in addition was considering his relationship to other publishers, particularly Göschen. At any rate, on April 19, 1805, he wrote Schiller about his connection with Göschen.

The memorandum which Goethe sent Cotta was dated May 1 and must have been drawn up by both men, since Goethe speaks of it as one "welches Herr Cotta schon kennt." To this document Goethe added a note agreeing to give Cotta the publication rights for from five to six years. For the edition he now demanded 10,000 taler, of which 1,000 was to be paid upon delivery of the first sheets of manuscript, the remainder in three successive installments at Easter of 1806, 1807, and 1808. The increase in payment which Goethe demanded can be explained in one of two ways, or both. The original honorarium was calculated from an estimated number of sheets. In the final reckoning Goethe probably discovered that the edition would be larger than he had thought. In addition we know from Schiller of his dislike of dealing *bogenweis*. He preferred to name a round sum. But there can be little doubt that the edition, calculating by sheets, would not have increased in size from 400 to 625, and we may assume that Goethe had simply decided to raise his price to see if Cotta would meet it.[3]

With the memorandum as a working basis, Cotta wrote

making certain emendations,[4] and Goethe, after some delay, returned to him on August 12, 1805, a document with comments on and reactions to these emendations ranged beside them.

Cotta offered to pay Goethe 10,000 taler and asked for rights for six years following publication. Goethe agreed, but extended the rights to eight years, in addition authorizing Cotta to publish a pocket edition if he so desired. Goethe also accepted Cotta's stipulation that the latter would succeed Göschen and Unger as his publisher, assuring Cotta that they no longer had any claims on his work. Cotta's final point stated that there should be no other new edition until this was completed. Goethe hedged on this, referring to his having extended the rights to eight years, and adding: "Damit sich der Autor nicht um die Stärcke der Auflage, nicht um die Weise zu bekümmern brauche wie der Verleger die Wercke ins Publikum bringt, ist dort eine Zeit festgesetzt, welche allen Misshelligkeiten vorbeugt."

Two days after the final arrangements about payment had been settled, Goethe wrote again, on September 30, sending the manuscript of *Wilhelm Meister,* giving further instructions, and preaching his familiar little sermon on typographical errors. He wanted samples of the proposed type and paper of the edition, and wished the physical aspect of the volumes to be as cheerful as possible. "Doch ist mir daran nicht so viel gelegen," he continued, "als an der Correctheit des Druckes. . . ." If there should by any remote chance be an error in the manuscript, he said, he would rather have it reproduced than allow anyone to make the slightest changes.

Cotta, complying with his author's wishes, sent the samples, about which Goethe was not at all enthusiastic. He suggested on November 25 that they were not as "modern und lustig" as one was accustomed to in northern Germany, and hinted that something more appropriate might be found. Again he reminded Cotta most emphatically to avoid errors, but tempered his tone somewhat by admitting that Cotta was not the only one who was plagued by difficulties of that sort.

He even managed to make a little joke about it, saying: "Hinter Bartholdy's Reisen, in der Real-[schul] buchhandlung zu Berlin gedruckt, stehen drey Blätter Druckfehler und man kann wohl sagen, dass dieser wackre Reisende von der Nachlässigkeit des Correctors mehr gelitten hat, als von allen Türken, Griechen und Arnauten zusammen. . . ."

For the first six or seven months of 1806 satisfaction reigned on both sides, marred only by two things—Goethe's continual reminders to Cotta that he avoid typographical errors, and the fear that Weimar would be plundered by the victorious French armies. Goethe displayed extraordinary tactlessness on the first point, saying on June 20: "Freylich wird es noch eine Zeitlang währen, bis die Süddeutschen Druckereyen in einer gewissen galanten Art den Norddeutschen gleich kommen." Cotta may have known Goethe well enough by this time not to take offense at such a statement, but it would be surprising if he was not annoyed.

On August 18 Goethe sent Cotta the manuscript for the fourth volume, with the exception of *Elpenor,* which he promised to have ready in the very near future. With the manuscript he sent a list of what was to appear in volumes 5-8. Writing again on October 20, he assured Cotta that his house had been miraculously spared from the plundering of the French, so that his papers were still intact. In spite of the confused political and military situation, the mail was apparently functioning fairly well, because on October 24 he said that the proofs of volume 4 had reached him. Cotta had evidently done his work carefully, since Goethe expressed himself as well satisfied with everything he had received thus far, a reaction which must have afforded the publisher some measure of relief.

Thinking perhaps that in such unsettled times Goethe might be in need of money, Cotta had generously offered him an advance on the next payment. This was one of Cotta's most appealing traits, and it would be doing him a great injustice to claim that he made such offers with a purely selfish end in view. Goethe seemed to be genuinely grateful for the offer of a helping hand, and replied on December 29, 1806, that he was deeply moved, but that for the time being he was making ends meet.

This friendly mood was not destined to last very long. Christmas must have been spoiled for both parties by an unfortunate occurrence for which Cotta was not wholly responsible. On December 25 Goethe had occasion to write to him, but not to send him the season's greetings nor to discuss the edition. He had noticed that in articles in the *Allgemeine Zeitung,* published by Cotta, someone had made remarks about Weimar and its citizens which were, in Goethe's opinion, "unschicklich und unanständig." There were two such articles, the first appearing in the *Allgemeine Zeitung,* No. 328, November 24, 1806. It deals with the aftermath of the battle of Jena and the subsequent occupation of Weimar by the French. That portion of it to which Goethe particularly objected ran as follows:

> Goethe liess sich unter dem Kanonendonner der Schlacht mit seiner vieljährigen Haushälterin, Dlle. Vulpius, trauen, und so zog sie allein einen Treffer, während viele Tausend Nieten fielen. Nur der Ununterrichtete kann darüber lächeln. Es war sehr brav von Goethe, der nichts auf gewöhnlichem Wege thut. Wieland erhielt vom Prinzen Joachim Murat aus freien Stücken eine Sauvegarde, und der Marschall Ney besuchte ihn selbst. Goethe hatte die Marschälle Lannes und Augereau, und dann den Kunstfreund Denon zu Gästen. Bertuch rettete sein grosses Institut gleichfalls durch liberale Bewirtung französischer Generäle, und indem er bewies, dass er die besten Erfindungen und Einrichtungen den Franzosen verdanke.

The second article came out in No. 352, December 18, 1806, and reads in part:

> Unserm famosen Romanfabrikanten Vulpius[5] ist es auch scharf ans Leben, und seiner Frau ans Nothzüchtigen gegangen; aber wenn es traurig ist, dergleichen zu erleben, so ist es eine Wonne, ihn die Scene erzählen zu hören. In jenen Momenten ist die Gebärmutter seines Geistes, aus der schon so viele Räuber und Ungeheuer hervor giengen, gewiss aufs neue zu einen

Dutzend ähnlicher Schöpfungen geschwängert worden, die in den nächsten Messen wie junge Ferkel herumgrunzen werden. Falk[6] macht den Galoppin bei den Stadtkommandanten, deren wir seit dem 14. Okt. schon vier angestellt hatten. Seine neueste Monatschrift wird dadurch wahrscheinlich ins Stocken gerathen, aber ich denke, das ist nicht der grösste Schade, den der Krieg über Deutschland gebracht hat, u.s.w.

Such scurrilous attacks could naturally not be taken lying down. We should be surprised and not a little disappointed if Goethe had not risen up in anger. Rather brusquely, he requested that Cotta act immediately to prevent a recurrence of such articles. In his letter of December 25 he said: "Halten Sie das Gute was wir zusammen noch vorhaben für bedeutend, fühlen Sie die Schönheit unsres Verhältnisses in seinem ganzen Umfang, so machen Sie diesen unwürdigen Redereyen ein Ende, die sehr bald ein wechselseitiges Vertrauen zerstören müssten. Nicht weiter!"

Cotta was naturally unhappy about the incident, as we can see from a subsequent letter of Goethe's of January 25, 1807, which referred to Cotta's reply. Goethe tried to be reasonable about the whole matter, but unfortunately hardly had he made this attempt when another report of the same type appeared and he was asked by higher-ups to protest to Cotta and send him for publication a refutation of certain remarks in the offending article.[7] As far as we know, the necessary steps were taken, since there is only one further reference to the matter in any subsequent correspondence,[8] and on February 2 Cotta told Böttiger that Goethe was at least reconciled towards him.[9]

Although Goethe was anxious to see his works in print in a collected edition, he could not muster much enthusiasm for his share of the responsibility. What he was about to publish was not new; much of it had already gone through more than one edition, and he had put it behind him as though it were a stage through which he had passed and now wished to forget. Had he been involved in something new and strange, it would have occupied his entire attention, but this was old and he had already got it out of his system and was tired of it.

But at the same time that he was occupied with the dull chores of revision and proofreading, he was compensating for this by working on new material. From what he said in a letter of November 1, we may assume that he had a definite plan in mind. While the public was awaiting new volumes of the collected works, he would hold its interest and keep his name before it by publishing articles.

Contrary to his procrastination over delivery of manuscript in his dealings with Göschen, he was able to supply Cotta with all he could handle, and on December 15, 1807, informed the publisher that he had sent, a week previously, the one missing volume of his works. But Cotta was slow in publishing the last eight volumes, and Goethe began to lose patience with him. By April 1808 he had still not received any copies and he told Zelter that he did not like Cotta's behavior. However, he had an idea that Cotta wanted to issue these eight volumes together, rather than in two issues of four each, as their agreement stipulated. He may well have been right, because from what he said to Zelter he had received only volumes 1-4. Since 5 and 7 are dated 1807 and the remaining six 1808, Cotta then must have printed two in 1807 and deliberately withheld them from the public—and from Goethe—until all eight were ready for distribution. The only other possibility is that Cotta printed all eight in 1808 and intentionally back-dated volumes 5 and 7 in case Goethe should accuse him of holding up publication for over a year, but this is scarcely credible in view of what we know about Cotta's integrity. His reasons for wishing to issue all eight volumes at once are not known; we can only assume that he felt that public interest would lag if too much time elapsed between the sale of the second and third parts of the edition. The final volumes apparently made their appearance sometime between April and December 1808.

In the two or three years following the completion of this edition, Goethe was concerned with the publication of four major works, but progress was extremely slow. The correspondence with Cotta during the years 1808-1811 is meager, to say the least. Material which would give us an idea of the negotiations with Cotta for the publication of *Die Wahlverwandtschaften* is sadly lacking. On March 2, 1809, Cotta wrote to Schiller's widow saying: ". . . Wenn doch Goethe mit seinem Roman herausrückte; anfangs sagte er's mir zu nun ist er wieder abgeneigt, ihn sogleich zu publiciren." Another reason for the paucity of correspondence may be found in Goethe's diary under the date April 21: "Die Wahlverwandtschaften. Dr. Cotta." It is altogether probable that during this visit of Cotta's to Weimar the matter was thrashed out in private discussion and the decision made to publish the book at Michaelmas 1809.

By October 1, 1809, the proofs of the second volume were ready, and Cotta thought that it was time to put the book on sale, since apparently pirated editions were already under way.[10] He must then have discussed with Goethe the possibility of using the novel as volume 13 of the recently completed edition, in addition to its sale as a separate work. Goethe raised no objections to this proposal, and volume 13 appeared in 1810. Until then there had been no mention of what Goethe was to be paid and he even claimed that he would not know how much to ask but would rely on Cotta's judgment and generosity.[11] There are no remarks about his remuneration in any correspondence, but in Cotta's accounts we find that on October 19, 1809, Goethe received another 500 taler.

As early as October 12, 1805, Goethe had told Zelter that it was his intention to have *Zur Farbenlehre* appear in the spring of the following year. Printing actually did begin during the winter, but Goethe realized immediately that it could not possibly be completed for another year. His favorite way of describing the work was "ein sisyphischer Stein." It is quite apparent that he was most anxious to have it out of the way. We have seen how he would lose interest in something that he had written many years before, and this is a similar case, where he had been occupied with these chromatic studies for so long. Then too, the dull chore of supervising the manuscript through the press was not something which he relished.

In the case of the *Farbenlehre,* and to a large extent, of all his scientific writings, he seemed far less concerned over publication than was true of his other works. One would think, in view of the exactness of the work and the number of technical terms involved, that Goethe would have been most particular about accuracy. If he was, then there is no indication of such concern; in fact, all the available evidence points in the other direction, though external distractions must also be taken into account. The threat of the French armies, along with the possible consequence that Weimar might be plundered and his papers destroyed, forced Goethe to publish as quickly as possible.

At the time that he was working on *Die Wahlverwandtschaften* and *Zur Farbenlehre* and immediately after their publication, Goethe was involved with three other works: *Philipp Hackert, Dichtung und Wahrheit,* and *Wilhelm Meisters Wanderjahre.* As in the case of *Die Wahlverwandtschaften,* there is little correspondence with the publisher about *Hackert.* We know that Cotta paid Goethe 400 taler for it in 1811.[12] Other correspondence reveals a good deal of confusion surrounding the negotiations with the Hackert heirs about the publication of the biography. If we consider for a moment why Goethe was so eager to have it published, we are forced to discard the idea that he needed the money. After all, he had just received 10,000 taler from Cotta for the collected works and 1,200 for the *Farbenlehre.* He was to receive only half of the 400 for *Hackert;* the remaining 200 was to go to the family. Apparently it was, then, a labor of love. As far back as May 11, 1808, he had made some suggestions to Hufeland about it. The latter, acting as intermediary between Goethe and the Hackert family, had given no answer until May 3, 1809, and his information was so discouraging that Goethe had decided to abandon the whole project. The Hackert family then relented somewhat, but there were so many conditions and stipulations attached that he still did not see his way clear to publication.[13] Then, sometime prior to March 5, 1810, the Hackerts again made overtures to Goethe, and on that date Goethe wrote Frommann, telling him that the outlook was more optimistic and advising him to buy Hackert's papers and to hand them over to him. He was anxious to find out what a reputable publisher could pay for such a manuscript, and also what the publisher would pay for having it edited by a man with an established reputation. The Hackert family must have accepted the terms which Goethe proposed, and the book finally appeared in 1811.

If we look back for a moment at the years 1807-1810, it seems, in the absence of evidence to the contrary, that they were years of comparative calm for Goethe and his publisher. Goethe, active in a literary way, was able to complete what he wanted to without any outside pressure. Cotta, intelligent enough to realize this, let him alone, not attempting to hurry him. Since as far as we know, there existed no ironclad contracts, Goethe may have passed the stage when he felt that he needed some sort of deadline to keep him at work. The *Wanderjahre* was the only book on which there was little progress, but neither author nor publisher felt that it should be rushed to completion. Goethe was contributing as regularly as he could to such journals and periodicals of Cotta's as the *Damen-Calender* and the *Allgemeine Zeitung,* so that Cotta had no reason to complain about lack of manuscript. All in all, during these years, their relations were perhaps as ideal as at any time during their long association.

Goethe's desire to see the *Wanderjahre* published was not to be realized until 1821, but the fact that he was not making progress on it did not seem to concern him, since he had already acquired a new interest, the writing of his autobiography. It is curious that from October 1, 1809, until March 31, 1811, there are in the Weimar Edition only two letters to Cotta. This fact, coupled with the very few letters of the years 1808 and 1809, could mean that there was correspondence which has been lost. On the other hand, if there are no more letters than we have, it is strange that in a period when three major works were either being written or published there was so little contact between author and publisher.

On October 25, 1810, Goethe wrote to Bettina Brentano, informing her of his intention to write his autobiography, and asking her to send him what memories she had of his youth. He had discussed his plan with Cotta in Jena on May 11. On November 16 he wrote that he still hoped the right moment would come along when he could bring himself to complete it.

The beginning of the work on *Dichtung und Wahrheit*, coming as it did so soon after the trials and tribulations of the publication of *Hackert*, and while he was still uncertain about the *Wanderjahre*, seemed like child's play for Goethe. He found it such an easy task that by September 7, 1811, he had sent Cotta the last part of Book 5, and with it the preface to Part I.[14]

The subject of a second edition of Goethe's collected works now arose, and for several months *Dichtung und Wahrheit* was relegated to a minor position.

On September 17, 1811, Cotta wrote that in order to give the pirates something to think about, he wished to publish an edition in small format.[15] This gave Goethe an opportunity to mention what had apparently been on his mind for some time, and on September 28 he answered that he would like to have additional information about such a plan before Cotta advertised the edition, since he had reservations on the subject. He thought that it would be much more effective and advantageous to go to work on a new, correct, and complete edition.

Suddenly the correspondence became more frequent and far livelier. The comparative quiet of the previous years was broken, and although one cannot go so far as to say that there was now a point of dissension between the two men, nevertheless the letters show a firm but also very polite attitude on both sides, with each speaking his mind unhesitatingly. Cotta did not agree with Goethe, and since the latter wished for more exact information, reminded him in a letter of October 1 that this edition had been planned eighteen months earlier and was now necessary because the octavo edition was almost sold out. He did not feel it advisable to think seriously about a complete edition.[16]

Goethe's reasons for not wishing to see a smaller edition published were fairly sound. He felt that a new complete edition would be of distinct financial advantage to him. But Cotta's reasons for objecting to a large edition were not stated. Perhaps he feared that the venture would not be financially successful. Goethe, of course, would have nothing to lose and everything to gain. He would stipulate and receive a fixed sum—and Cotta would pay it regardless of any losses he himself might incur; it was possible that there would be losses. Goethe may have realized this—at any rate, in his next letter, written on October 14, he used two arguments, one calculated to have its effect on Cotta's sense of business ethics, the other quite personal. First, he reminded Cotta that in 1805 their agreement stipulated that the small edition appear fairly soon after the large one. Even when a year and a half had passed and Cotta mentioned the subject, Goethe said that he had raised no objections. But now, when the termination of Cotta's rights was so close at hand, the publication of a cheap edition would prolong indefinitely the appearance of a new complete one. He then went on to a more personal matter: "Diese meine Verlegenheit wird noch dadurch vermehrt, dass die Meinigen, denen ich, in Betracht der Vergänglichkeit eines menschlichen Individuums, von meinen oekonomischen Verhältnissen Notiz zu geben gewohnt bin, dieses Ereigniss mit einer besondern *Ombrage* betrachten, welche zu mildern ich mich nicht im Stande sehe. Vielleicht entspringen diese Besorgnisse aus einer Unkenntniss des Handelsganges und würden bey mündlicher wechselseitiger Erklärung wohl gehoben werden können."

We know that Cotta wrote again on November 2, 1811, and from what Goethe said in his reply of November 16 the publisher must have suggested that his rights to the edition of 1806-1808 be extended. Goethe then became very business-like, and took it upon himself to send Cotta a resumé of the agreement reached in 1805 prior to publication. He prefaced this by saying that their business relationship could only be seen clearly in their letters, since no real contract had ever been drawn up. Then followed the summary, each point ending with the remark that 1814 remained the date for the termination of Cotta's rights. Since Cotta apparently thought that the later inclusion of *Die Wahlverwandtschaften* as volume 13 entitled him to an extension of his publishing privileges, Goethe bluntly stated: "Dass nun in der Folge, auf Antrag des Herrn Verlegers, die Wahlverwandtschaften als 13. Band abgedruckt wurden kann keine Änderung machen. Der Verfasser willigte unter dem Zusatz ein, dass es damit wie mit dem Uebrigen gehalten werde. Welche Worte wohl keine andre Auslegung erleiden, als dass das Verlags-Recht auch dieses Bandes sich bis Ostern 1814 erstrecken solle." This whole letter was obviously designed to show Cotta that Goethe was determined to hold him to the agreements reached in 1805. Cotta might well have thought of Schiller's warning: "Liberalität gegen seine Verleger ist seine Sache nicht."

The subject was then left hanging fire for almost three months. Possibly each man thought that the other might be inclined to yield if given time to reconsider. In his reply of March 7, Cotta, worried about piracy, brought the subject up again, saying: "Was ich in Ihrem Schreiben aber am meissten vermisste, war die Erklärung wegen der Werke—wir geben den Nachdruckern gewonnen Spiel, wenn mit einer wolfeilen Ausgabe länger gezaudert wird—bereits meldet man mir von Berlin, dass der Wiener Nachdruk sich dort einschliche."[17] Goethe's answer of March 17 appears at first sight to show a drastic change of heart. He said that he had more or less misunderstood Cotta's intentions and was awaiting suggestions. Then, referring probably to Cotta's remark about the danger of the pirated edition from Vienna, he said: "Denn da ich den technischen und merkantilischen Theil solcher Unternehmungen nicht verstehe, so wüsste ich nicht zu finden wie der mir drohende grosse Schade dabey abzuwenden?" This sounds very much as if he was saying: "You know best," and giving in to Cotta. For the first time he admitted to a publisher that he knew little or nothing about the business end of the publishing profession, and with all due respect to Goethe one finds it hard to believe that he actually meant it. But his statements are all vague. He did not say in the letter whether he approved of a cheaper edition. Instead, he went on to tell the publisher what a hard time he was having trying to justify his request for a new one. He reminded Cotta that the advantages which might accrue to either one of them would of necessity affect the other. He said that he had never before given much thought to advantages (and we may assume that he used the word in a financial sense). The letter continued: "Und doch muss ich daran dencken, wenn ich nicht nach einem mühsamen und mässigen Leben verschuldet von der Bühne abtreten will. Der Augenblick zehrt schon wieder an unserm Marck, Freunde und Bekannte fallen um mich her, niemand kann dem andern beystehn. Doch wozu reden und klagen! Nur diesmal erlaubt ich mirs um Sie zu überzeugen dass mein Zaudern nicht aus veränderten Gesinnungen, sondern aus den veränderten Umständen sich herschreibe." Somehow this letter does not ring true. It is too wordy without coming to a definite conclusion, and while the first part seems acquiescent, the second does not agree with it. We know that Goethe could write letters which said virtually nothing, or at least contained remarks which were so indefinite as to be of little value. What he really said to Cotta here was that he needed money. It is true that another complete edition of his works would be good advertising for Cotta; perhaps that is what Goethe meant when he said that his profits were Cotta's too. But, on the other hand, there was no real assurance that Cotta would gain financially from such a venture.

Cotta was evidently still not convinced, and he may well have decided that they were not making any progress by prolonging their correspondence, for on April 17 he visited Goethe in Weimar to discuss the edition. Money must have been one of the main topics of conversation, because in his letter of May 10 Goethe began by deploring the fact that their common friend Schiller was no longer at hand to take care of the unpleasant financial negotiations. Their meeting had apparently been unsatisfactory, so that Goethe felt himself forced to tell Cotta by letter what he had not told him personally. The point of friction turned out to be the remuneration for *Dichtung und Wahrheit,* and Goethe simply sent his publisher an ultimatum on May 10, 1812: "Ich kann nämlich meine biographischen Arbeiten vorerst nicht weiter publiciren, wenn Ew. Wohlgeb. den Band nicht mit zweytausend Thalern honoriren können, so dass ich auch auf den ersten fünfhundert Thaler Nachschuss erhielte. Ich beziehe mich auf alles was ich früher über meine Lage eröffnet und füge nur soviel hinzu: dass abermals dringende Umstände meine Erklärung beschleunigen mit der ich ungern hervortrete." Just what these pressing circumstances were, we do not know, but it is no secret that Christiane was costing him a good deal. In addition, his son August was being educated at the time, and the war may have cost Goethe something. But on the other hand he could afford to go to Carlsbad to take the waters. Trying to drive a hard bargain was characteristic of Goethe, as we know, and he generally got what he wanted. He was successful this time, too; on May 23 Cotta wrote that he would meet Goethe's demands.[18]

For fourteen months now there was almost complete silence. Cotta was no doubt somewhat put out by Goethe's attitude, and hence did not write; and Goethe, temporarily satisfied by Cotta's agreement, decided to rest on his laurels and work on his autobiography and material for the forthcoming edition.

Along with *Dichtung und Wahrheit* and the preparation for the new edition, Goethe had yet another iron in the fire: the *Italienische Reise.* He told Riemer on June 23 that he had thought of beginning publication in July. Now he told Cotta on July 19 that he expected to be ready with it in September when he returned from his summer holiday. In addition, he was prepared to offer him a *Vorspiel für Halle* and an occasional poem for immediate publication in the *Damen-Calen-*

der or *Morgenblatt*. One gets the impression here that he was most anxious to have done with as many details as possible before leaving for Carlsbad. Actually, his plans and propositions rarely materialized on time, as we have seen. But he was going through an extraordinarily active period—not only as far as publication was concerned. The correspondence of these years indicates how large his circle of acquaintances was and how many variegated interests he had. One wonders how he found the time to take care of all his letters and to continue his own work at the same time. Towards Cotta he seemed to be in a most expansive mood, following his successful negotiations for the new edition and the large sum for *Dichtung und Wahrheit*.

Goethe began the editing and correcting for the new edition long before a contract was drawn up and signed. He felt that by November 1814 the manuscript for the first six volumes would be ready for the press and informed Cotta that he would allow him publishing rights for seven years, beginning at Easter 1815. As usual, he was far too optimistic, because the first four volumes were not sent to Stuttgart until March 27, 1815. Negotiations for the sum which he expected to receive had actually begun on December 21, 1814, when he approached Cotta very politely and tentatively. He avoided particularly any phrasing which might give the impression of a demand. But we know enough of his business methods by now, and Cotta probably had learned enough too, to realize that when Goethe made a "suggestion" about remuneration, he had made up his mind that that was what he was going to get. The only adjustment in his figures would have been up, not down. In introducing the subject of his stipend to Cotta, he said: "Zuvörderst will ich meine Hoffnung und Erwartung nicht verhehlen, dass der Vortheil, den mir diese Ausgabe bringen möchte, demjenigen wenigstens proportionirt sey, den mir die vorige gebracht, und da ich diessmal mich zu zwanzig Bänden verpflichten kann, so würde wohl auch hiernach der Maasstab anzulegen seyn." Then, cleverly avoiding a direct statement as to what he wished to receive, he veered off on a more personal tack. He went on to say that this might well be the last time that he could enjoy the fruits of his whole life's work, and that he was all the more anxious to do this because of having heard of the public's great desire to purchase his complete works. After explaining further to Cotta that many people, particularly the youth of the country, looked up to him and were trying to educate themselves through him, he concluded by saying that he felt 16,000 taler might be appropriate for what he had to offer.

Goethe sent the rough draft of a contract to Cotta on February 20. Accompanying this was an announcement for public consumption and a tentative table of contents for the twenty volumes. This rough draft remained practically unchanged—in other words, Cotta agreed to all six points which Goethe made.

Cotta declared himself ready and willing to begin printing operations almost immediately, and on March 27 Goethe sent him the material for the first four volumes. In June he traveled to Wiesbaden to take the waters, and from there sent on the 15th the final contract with his signature. The first installment of the edition was ready, but Cotta was holding it back, waiting until the political situation was more settled before opening his subscription list. On December 6 Goethe made a unique proposal, the gist of which was that the public be permitted to buy, if they so desired, only those volumes of this new twenty-volume edition which contained material not in their older twelve-volume sets. This was a device calculated to please everyone—author, publisher, and public. For those who possessed the first Cotta edition and were not likely to want another, it enabled them to add to their libraries without duplication. In other words, where people might have balked at a new edition and bought nothing, by this means they would at least buy about half the volumes, thus assuring the publisher of greater profits and the author of wider circulation.

On January 10, 1816, Goethe sent Cotta the sixth volume and the revised and corrected version of *Was wir bringen* to complete the fifth, and at the same time he was busy preparing the *Italienische Reise* for publication. He was now in a period of tremendous activity. By June 26 he had the eleventh and twelfth volumes of the collected works ready, in addition to the first part of the *Italienische Reise*. He informed Cotta that once these were published he would be finished with the second part of the *Italienische Reise* and the fourth part of *Dichtung und Wahrheit*. Goethe was also prepared to present to the public the collection of articles on *Organische Bildung*. He had other works ready too, but told Cotta that it would perhaps be wiser to leave them untouched for a time. Possibly his grief over the death of Christiane was in part responsible for this surge of activity. He may have tried to overcome the pain by working, and it perhaps too brought to his mind the thought that he himself might not have much longer to live. This could explain the urge to see his work in print as soon as possible.

We have noticed how, since the time of the final agreement concerning the publication of this edition, there had been no friction between publisher and author. Cotta had not complained about Goethe's financial demands, nor had he pressed him for material. Goethe, for his part, had sent no carping letters and had been as good as his word in keeping Cotta supplied with manuscript, both for the edition and for sundry periodicals. He was manifestly pleased with the way work was progressing, and on October 22 wrote praising the type and quality of paper.

By December 16 he had sent to his publisher fourteen volumes of the works, and promised the two next volumes by the first of the year. He was as good as his word, and on January 7, 1817, mailed a kind of progress report, telling him that volumes 15 and 16 had been sent and that the last four would be on their way by Easter. However, he had great difficulty in filling these out. In fact, he eventually had to remove material from six other volumes in order to make up the 14th.[19] This delayed completion of the edition long past Easter, and as late as July 6 he was still undecided as to how to finish it. On that date he wrote Cotta that *Rameaus Neffe* would be the first work in volume 20, but that the rest was still indefinite. On September 6 he asked how much more material was needed to complete volume 20. We see his desire to get this edition out of the way so that his work would be in a permanent form when he mentioned to Cotta the fact that Tieck was anxious for a contribution to his proposed *Musen-Almanach.* "Ich habe," he wrote, "unzählige Anmuthungen dieser Art mit den günstigsten Anerbieten, ich lehne aber alles ab, weil ich meine Arbeit nicht zersplittern und unser Verhältniss nicht beeinträchtigen mag."

Since Cotta's efforts to obtain privileges in Austria to protect his Goethe edition had been unsuccessful, he had discovered another plan by which he thought piracy in that country could be prevented. On September 28 he wrote asking permission to send a copy of all freshly printed material to Vienna so that it could be copied and censored there as manuscript. This was, he claimed, the only way of preventing further piracy.[20] Goethe replied on October 25 that this device was new to him, but he felt that it would be easy to follow the plan. The importance lay in the fact that the manuscript should be censored in Vienna. Just how this operated Cotta did not explain, but we can assume that the task of obtaining privileges was greatly simplified.[21]

Following Cotta's return from a trip to Italy, Goethe wrote in a very friendly fashion on May 10, 1818, welcoming him home. Again he could give Cotta a report on how best to fill out the last volume of their edition. To do this he had decided to take material already published in the ill-starred *Propyläen.* This is the last we hear of the second edition of Goethe's collected works published by Cotta. Goethe's fears that this was to be the final edition which he would live to see proved groundless.

The *West-östlicher Divan,* published in 1819, had taken years to prepare. As early as December 16, 1816, Goethe told Frommann that he felt the poems were ready for publication, but work progressed very slowly. On December 21, 1817,

Goethe sent Frommann the manuscript of the first book, but it was not until September 26, 1818, that he could tell Boisserée that the poems were printed. Even now, however, the book was not to appear, since he thought that notes and explanations were necessary in order to make the poems comprehensible to those who knew little or nothing of the Orient. Revision and correction dragged on and on; Goethe told Sartorius on April 4, 1819, that the snail's pace of the printer was unbearable. On May 26 he wrote his son that things were still going far too slowly, and in July he went to Jena in order to try and speed up the process. He may have met with some success, because he said to Cotta on August 11: "Der 'Divan' ist nun endlich beisammen, und ich bin sehr zufrieden, diese Arbeit los zu seyn, die sich im Fortschreiten auf manche Weise immer schwieriger machte."

We will have more to say about the *Divan* in the following chapter, where it figures prominently in a situation which led to some unpleasantness between Goethe and Cotta.

The last important individual publication which we shall mention here is *Wilhelm Meisters Wanderjahre*. We have seen that Goethe's plan to publish it in 1810 was unsuccessful; it was not until December 9, 1820, that he sent Frommann the first batch of manuscript. Of the eight stories in the *Wanderjahre*, five had appeared prior to 1821 in "Taschenbücher." We have mentioned elsewhere the difficulty Goethe had in filling out his novel for its inclusion in the collected works.

There is little enough to say about this particular publication. At first the work proceeded too slowly for Goethe's liking, since he felt that it would prevent his leaving on his annual trip to take the cure, but by June the work was complete and Goethe had begun to send out his gift copies.

With the publication of the *Wanderjahre* we come to the end of the major individual works published in book form. We have seen that these publications fall into three fairly well-defined periods, 1800-1804, 1808-1815, 1818-1822. Each period is separated from the following one by the publication of an edition of Goethe's collected works, and from what has been said, we see that Goethe was most active in each of these three periods. It is also evident that his relationship with Cotta was for the most part extremely cordial. The only recurrence of his old domineering attitude is the demand for more money if his autobiography was to be continued. As we have already hinted, the reason for this relatively happy state of affairs was that Goethe was not under pressure from his publisher. When he wished to complete a work and have it published, he was able to do so when he so desired, not because he felt he was under compulsion to meet a deadline or fulfil the terms of a contract. Formality, in the business sense of the word, was at a minimum, and at such times Goethe felt himself less bothered by the old specter of the publishing world than when the relationship was on a more formal basis.

Goethe's activity in publishing these individual works can be explained. In more than one case he probably found himself in need of money, since it is no secret that he liked to live well. His menus and wine bills show that he ate and drank the best. However, the expenses of maintaining a home and family should not be overrated. By far the most important reasons in his mind were, first of all, the irresistible urge to see his work in print, in a form which he felt would last and be preserved for posterity, and second, the fact that he began to feel his years and wonder how much longer he might live.

We cannot help noticing that only once did he make use of an intermediary for publication of these works. Possibly Frommann may at times have acted in that capacity, but if so, only incidentally. He was never a Bertuch or Schiller or Boisserée. Why, we might ask ourselves, did Goethe not find it convenient to have a mediator? One may perhaps answer that, following the death of Schiller, Goethe had no one to whom he felt he could turn for assistance in negotiating with his publisher. This might possibly be true of the period following the publication of the first Cotta edition, since he did not make Boisserée's acquaintance until May 1811. However, at the time the second edition appeared, the two were firm friends, and Goethe could certainly have counted upon Boisserée's help had he asked for it. The answer probably lies in the fact that there was relatively little financial haggling over these publications. Only in the case of *Dichtung und Wahrheit* did Goethe make an issue of money, and then Cotta gave in with very little resistance. He may have realized that this was the most salable book which Goethe had produced for some time. If, as Goethe stated, he needed the money urgently, he probably did not have time to search for someone to convey his wishes to Cotta, and the exigencies of the situation overcame his natural dislike for financial dickering.

Before proceeding to the *Ausgabe letzter Hand,* let us see whether anything definitive can be said about Goethe's relationship to Cotta on the basis of what we now know about the publication of the collected works of 1806-1808 and 1816-1818. Obviously Goethe felt a distinct difference between an undertaking such as the publication of twelve or twenty volumes, and an isolated volume here and there. In other words, the problems connected with a complete edition called for a very much more formal approach. The size of the task and the amount of money involved made him feel that he had to be far more exact and far more exacting. For the second edition there was a formal contract rather than an exchange of letters. The remarks about format and type appeared once again, as did the constant reminders to be careful about misprints. He began to think more seriously about the problem of piracy. All of these things were lacking in the interim periods.

There can be no doubt that the publication of these two editions, particularly the second, was something which meant much to Goethe. There is a strong possibility that he felt that whereas isolated publications might be scattered and lost, a set of the complete works was something which was far more permanent, and after all, this was most important to him. It could account partly for his being as careful and particular as he was. In addition, the large sums of money involved were most attractive, and, to give him his due, he felt that if he and Cotta were going to profit by these ventures, the public should have something worth while for its money. He was determined to give them what he had pledged himself to give. That can be pointed out in the case of all three Cotta editions as well as that published by Göschen.

But the similarity between his reactions to the Göschen edition and those of Cotta ends there. Gone was the commanding tone, the domineering and downright rude manner of commenting on work done or not done. Not that Goethe had relaxed his standards or become any less determined to drive a hard bargain. But there was a very discernible change. With Cotta he tried persuasion and argument instead of orders, although there is no denying that he was firm and unyielding. He must have realized, as we hinted in speaking of the beginning of this relationship, that here was a man who was unlike other publishers, who could not be handled in the same way as Göschen, Unger, Vieweg, and other lesser lights of the profession.

And yet—and there seems to be an "and yet" with almost every phase of Goethe's relationship to the publishing world—this more lenient, more appreciative attitude was not to last. The old hard-headed, distrustful Goethe was merely lying dormant, soon to awaken.

Chapter 4

I

"Zugleich vermelde dass ich so eben beschäftigt bin, meine sämmtlichen poetischen, literarischen und wissenschaftlichen Arbeiten, sowohl gedruckte als ungedruckte, übersichtlich aufzustellen, sodann aber das Ganze meinem Sohne und einem geprüften gelehrten Freunde in die Hände zu legen, damit der weitläufige und in manchem Sinne bedenkliche Nachlass in's Klare komme und auch von dieser Seite mein Haus bestellt sey." Thus Goethe wrote to Cotta on April 19, 1822, and it is the first hint at what was eventually to become the last edition of his works to be published during his lifetime. Whether Cotta interpreted his words to mean that Goethe was planning another edition is not known. At any rate, on June 8 Goethe wrote to Friedrich von Luck,[1] telling him of his intentions, but asking him to keep them a secret for the time being. At the same time he divulged the information to Schultz.[2] Von Henning[3] also received a letter with the news, as Goethe told him that to attempt the correction and revision of his entire literary output by himself would be "Verwegenheit," and asked him on June 13 if he would assume responsibility for the scientific works on color and possibly all of the work in the physical sciences.

Not until September 8 did Goethe give his publisher any further information as to his intentions, and even then he kept his wording indefinite enough so as not to have Cotta jump to any conclusions. He told him of the "Repositur" which his friends had created during his summer absence, and wrote: ". . . ich verhandele nun mit meinen älteren und jüngeren Freunden, wie davon Gebrauch zu machen seyn möchte und wie, wenn ich auch abgerufen würde, doch nichts verloren seyn dürfte." If Cotta guessed what Goethe had in mind, he was obviously not going to be hurried into making an offer, and he may have had good reasons too, as we shall see shortly. Each seemed to have something which he wanted kept from the other, and it was as though they were sparring cautiously, each hoping the other would make the first move.

However, by May 7, 1823, Goethe had made up his mind, since he told Schultz, who seems to have been the leader of the so-called *Verein* which was assisting him, that he would be extremely grateful if this group would work towards a complete edition of his writings and that he would appreciate advice and suggestions. The work of the *Verein* was of great assistance, but it was not enough. Goethe was in the process of making what Houben calls "sein literarisches Testament,"[4] and the material with which and out of which he was working had accumulated to a point where it was beyond his control. The friends who agreed to help him, among them Schultz, von Henning, von Reinhard, Göttling, and Döbereiner were willing to do their best, but they were scattered throughout the country and were moreover occupied with the duties of their own positions. They could devote only their leisure hours to the correction and revision of Goethe's works, and he could do no more than ask them to assist him. He could not command their services.

And so we see Goethe reaching out into the world about him, searching for a person to whom he could entrust the task of making order out of the mass of material which was to become the *Ausgabe letzter Hand*. The result of this search was the discovery of a secretary, friend, and amanuensis, Johann Peter Eckermann. Eckermann was not the first younger man whom Goethe considered; Schubarth, a tutor in Berlin, Zauper, a professor at Pilsen, and Adrian, later to be known in connection with Heine's works in his capacity as censor in Giessen, were others whom he had in mind.

It was not until late in 1823 that something occurred which forced Cotta to suggest that he publish a new edition of Goethe's complete works. Goethe had spent the summer of 1823 in Carlsbad, and while there had made an ominous discovery, about which he wrote to Cotta on September 21, following his return to Weimar.

Ich fand mich nämlich im Buchladen, zum eisernen Kreuz in Carlsbad, mit mehreren Freunden und Fremden, denen man eine Ausgabe meiner Wercke, Wien und Stuttgart, den letzten Band vom vorigen Jahre, unbewunden vorlegte.[5] Man war im Handel und fragte mich was denn wohl von dem vorliegenden Abdruck zu halten sey? Ich antwortete, vielleicht zu naiv: dass ich gar nichts davon wisse! Und bey näherer Betrachtung musste es doch bedencklich scheinen, eine *Original Ausgabe* wovon der Verfasser keine Kenntniss hat und der Verleger sich nicht nennt, vor Augen zu sehen. Sodann überzeugte mich nur weniges Nachblättern dass hier die krassesten Druckfehler der ersten Abdrücke abermals vervielfältigt und gleichsam verewigt worden.

Anwesende fragten mich ferner; wie es denn komme, dass man die ächte Ausgabe nur bis zum 20ten Theil, diesen Nachdruck aber bis zum 26ten vorfinde? Wodurch die Besitzer der ersten sehr benachtheiligt wären. Welche Frage ich denn auch nicht genugsam zu beantworten im Stande, in meiner eigensten Sache als gleichgültig, nachlässig und unvorsichtig erscheinen musste.

Haben Sie die Güte mich darüber aufzuklären zu meiner Beruhigung: denn ich darf wohl versichern dass es der einzige unangenehme Eindruck ist den ich von meinem heurigen, sonst so glücklichen Sommeraufenthalt mit nach Hause bringe. Alles Weiteren enthalt ich mich, und darf die Versicherung kaum hinzufügen: dass sich für mich selbst, so lange mir hier zu verweilen gegönnt ist als auch künftig für die Meinigen, das so werthe, zwischen uns bestehende Verhältniss, welches mich immer an die Vermittlung Schillers erinnert, immer fort ungetrübt sich erhalten möge.

Cotta was every bit as upset about this as Goethe, and his explanation was perfectly credible. However, what hurt Goethe most was the fact that he had not been apprised of the situation. For him to have to discover the edition purely by chance was in his eyes a breach of faith on the part of his publisher.

In order to understand Cotta's reply we must know something about the relationship between Cotta and Armbruster. The latter had come into contact with Cotta through his father, J. M. Armbruster, who wished to help his son find a place in the publishing world. The suggestion was made in 1810 that, in order to head off the Austrian pirates, Cotta allow young Armbruster to publish an edition of Goethe's works in Vienna.[6] Cotta agreed, and the correspondence between the two men began in earnest shortly after the ruling regarding piracy of works censored in Vienna had been passed. Armbruster went into partnership with Christian Kaulfuss, but it was a long time before work on the Goethe edition began, nor was there, up until 1814, much of a campaign by the two publishers against piracy. In the autumn of 1814 Cotta and his family came to Vienna, as a result of his decision to begin, with Bertuch, operations against the Austrian pirate publishers. Bertuch, because of illness, withdrew at the last moment, and sent his son Karl in his stead. He proved so efficient that in 1815 Cotta returned home, leaving the young man to carry on, and it was due to his untiring efforts that a paragraph dealing with freedom of the press and piracy was inserted into the records of the Congressional proceedings.

The first mention of the Goethe edition in Armbruster's correspondence with Cotta was on November 13, 1815, when he suggested that Cotta allow him to publish a notice in order to discourage pirates. Goethe, as we know, agreed on March 25, 1816, to the publication of an edition in Vienna. By May 22 enough progress had been made for Armbruster to tell Cotta that his decision to publish a Goethe edition in Vienna had caused a sensation and that he was sure the plan would work out. It was highly probable that the edition would have every chance of success, since it was priced at 40 florins, while the pirates had been charging 100. On May 22 Armbruster had received the manuscript of the first two volumes and had managed to have them passed by the censor.

And so the way was cleared and printing began. On October 23, 1819, Armbruster wrote to Cotta that volume 20 was about to come off the press. He urged Cotta to publish another volume, warning him that some pirate would if he did not. As a result of this letter, and the fact that a pirate

86

had already asked for permission to publish the *Divan,* Cotta allowed Armbruster to include it as the twenty-first volume of the edition, originally planned in twenty volumes. When the publisher informed the authorities of his intentions, permission was immediately granted by virtue of the ruling of October 12, 1810.

This is apparently all the information obtainable from the archives. It is unfortunate that it goes no farther, since nothing is said about the five following volumes which Armbruster published, and which were the real bone of contention between Goethe and Cotta. However, turning now to Cotta's letter of explanation to Goethe, we can perhaps fill out the remaining events. According to that letter, Cotta was not inclined to allow Armbruster to publish more than the twenty volumes. He wrote Goethe on October 18, 1823:

Nun erhalte ich als der Divan, glaube ich, erschienen einen 21sten Band mit der Entschuldigung gegen meine Protestation, dass er, Armbruster, hiezu genöthigt worden sey, weil sonst andre österreichische Buchhändler diss Werk, worauf sie schon bei der Censurstelle eingekommen, nachdruken, seine Ausgaben dadurch verderben und eine frühere von Geistinger veranstaltete die wegen der Armbrusterschen nicht fortgesetzt werden durfte sonst von der Censur hiezu legitimirt worden wäre—ich replicirte, dass er wenigstens meine Vollmacht dazu hätte haben müssen dass ich gegen jedes weitere ähnliche Einschreiten mich verwahre—allein er hatte meine Fonds, ich war in seinen Händen und dergleichen Processe sind schwer zu schlichten—So streiten wir selbst über das, was ich an ihn an Capital zu seiner Etablirung aus Freundschaft ihm vorschoss, und was wenigstens Erkentlichkeit hätte erwerben sollen, seit Jahr und Tag—also über mein eigentliches Eigenthum. Es gibt nichts bittereres und unangenehmeres als was ich an diesem Menschen erfahren habe und ich habe die Sache nun auf einen schiedsrichterlichen Spruch ausgesetzt. Das Beste wird seyn, bald auf eine neue weitzuverbreitende Ausgabe zu denken. Ich erwarte Ihre Verfügung und bald ein paar beruhigende Worte.[7]

There is no doubt that Cotta was genuinely unhappy at what Armbruster had done. He had a great deal of money tied up in this venture and apparently could not afford to lose it. Whether he could have fought Armbruster more energetically is a question we cannot answer. There was also a hint of blackmail where Armbruster was concerned, because although Cotta's paper, *Die Allgemeine Zeitung,* was permitted to circulate in Austria, its footing was by no means sure, since the tone of some articles was not quite to the liking of the government. In 1815 Armbruster had told Cotta: ". . . ich besorge (nicht *ohne Grund*), dass Ihre Zeitung, wenn sie in dem angezeigten Tone fortfahren sollte, zuverlässig bei uns *verboten* werden wird." This warning came from Hofrat von Ohms, with whom Armbruster was on fairly good terms. Perhaps Armbruster meant, and Cotta realized, that the former would persuade von Ohms to ban *Die Allgemeine Zeitung* if Cotta did not co-operate with him. Hence it is possible that Cotta, in order to keep his paper alive in Austria, pirated himself in Austria (through Armbruster) to the extent of six volumes of Goethe's collected works.[8]

None of this came to Goethe's attention, but for him the really important part of Cotta's letter was not so much the explanation but the suggestion that a new, complete edition of his works be published. Hence it was that shortly thereafter, on November 5, Goethe could write to Schultz and tell him that the subject of a new edition had been taken up with Cotta, who was agreeable to the idea. Goethe may well have wished that Cotta should be the one to make the overtures, hence his hesitation in confiding in him sooner, but it is doubtful whether he thought that the incident mentioned above would be the starting-point. Nevertheless, from the tone of the letter in which he accepted Cotta's explanations, one is inclined to think that he was so relieved that the publisher had finally made the first move that he glossed over the incident in order to be able to get to more serious business, but he did not simply dismiss the whole affair as an unfortunate oversight on Cotta's part. He naturally had something to say about it, although one has the impression that he was already preoccupied with a more pressing problem. Rather than accuse Cotta directly of not being quite honest with him, he veiled his statements very thinly by generalizing, as we can see from his answer, written on January 14, 1824:

Die Erläuterungen, die Sie mir über einen, uns beiden höchst unangenehmen Punct ertheilen, mussten freylich alle die schmerzlichen Gefühle auf einmal wieder erregen, an die ein deutscher Autor Zeit seines lebens nur allzuoft erinnert wird und welche diessmal den verdüsterten Geist so schwarz als möglich umhüllten.

Denn indem der Schriftsteller manchen, der seine eingeborene Kraft und Fähigkeit zu löblichen Zwecken folgerecht verwendet, prosperiren, und auch wohl im Alter mit Gütern gesegnet sieht, so muss er, der sich's eifrig angelegen seyn liess seine eigene Bildung und wo möglich die des Vaterlands zu steigern, sich auf mannichfaltige Weise verletzt und um die billige Belohnung seiner unausgesetzten Arbeiten getäuscht sehen.

That was all that was said on the subject. Perhaps Goethe meant that his relationship with Cotta had hitherto been so satisfactory that he had begun to forget his old grievances against the publishing profession. But now suddenly all the mistrust and unpleasant experiences of the past became real again. There is another possibility which we may bear in mind: perhaps this incident of the Vienna "pirated" edition made him drive such a hard bargain with Cotta when it came to a contract for the *Ausgabe letzter Hand,* and which played its part in Goethe's attitude in connection with the publication of his correspondence with Schiller.[9] We shall see how, as soon as negotiations began, Goethe seemed bent upon getting the better of Cotta. He was, of course, influenced by his son August, who, although he may have been a better businessman than his father, did not help relations between him and his publisher.

But to return to Goethe's letter. He did not press the matter further, and plunged into a discussion of the new edition. Naturally one of the first points which he brought up was the matter of payment. His method of approaching the topic was one which he had used before: mentioning it in rather formal terminology and saying that of course Cotta was the only one who would be able to arrange matters satisfactorily, but there can have been little doubt in Goethe's mind that he, and not Cotta, would have the last word where money was involved, and he adopted this approach in order to draw Cotta out.

We come now to a point which has already been mentioned, namely, the ever-increasing emphasis in Goethe's correspondence with Cotta on the welfare of his family. He had begun to realize that, although he and they had never wanted for those things which made for a comfortable, if not luxurious, existence, he had relatively little which he could bequeath to them when he died. Unless he could make sure that a steady income from the sale of his writings would be available to his children after his death, they would soon use up what there was on hand and then find themselves in an embarrassing financial position. The desire to spare his family this unpleasantness, in addition to his determination to drive as hard a bargain as possible, gave rise to two protracted sets of negotiations, one with Cotta, the other with the parliament.

He was not expecting an easy time with Cotta once serious discussions of terms started, and this may well have discouraged him from immediate negotiations. Having accepted Cotta's explanation of the Armbruster edition he asked for proposals as to the next step. Cotta did not answer promptly, and when he did, on February 15, made only rather general statements about the edition. No doubt he had good reason for wishing to put it out of his mind for a while, since he was busy just then getting married for the second time.[10] Goethe was tactful enough to take cognizance of this event and did not communicate again with Cotta until May 30, but he was none the less occupied with supervision of the work being done by Eckermann and the *Verein*. The spring also saw the beginning of another venture—one which was to lead him perilously close to a complete break with Cotta—the publication of his correspondence with Schiller.

On May 30, 1824, Goethe felt that it was time to mention the subject of the edition again to Cotta, particularly since he thought that considerable progress had been made. His archive had been rounded into form so that his son and other co-workers knew now where almost everything was to be found. He had also been able to proceed with what he called the "Chronik meines Lebens." Until April 4, 1825, we have no further correspondence between the two. We may ask what busied Goethe during those eleven months to such an extent that he found no time to communicate with his publisher. The answer is that he was energetically carrying on a successful campaign to win for himself what amounted to a copyright for his works. This would, of course, eliminate pirated editions, and by virtue of his contract with Cotta, provide for his children after his death.

II

It was during his association with Göschen that Goethe first showed any real sign of anxiety about piracy, and it will perhaps not be amiss to digress from our main topic here to say something about his reactions to it. At the time, he was certainly not ignorant of the fact that his works had been and were still being pirated. But this had apparently left him quite undisturbed. In 1785, planning a present for the Gräfin Brühl, he wrote the following to Reich on August 22: "Ersuche um die Gefälligkeit die beste Ausgabe meiner Schrifften, in vier Bänden, in schönem englischen Band mit grünem Schnitt, binden zu lassen und mir solche wohlgepackt zu übersenden." In all probability this edition of which he wrote was Himburg's third pirated edition, actually a most elegant one in comparison to the usual cheap pirated works. We can see how very unconcerned he was about this sort of thing. But a year later he seemed to become alive to the fact that he was suffering real harm.

His apparent nonchalance about piracy and lack of action against pirates stemmed partly from the fact that he knew he could do nothing to stop them. He was well informed about such evil practices; the journals and periodicals of his day were full of arguments and suggestions on the subject. But all that he did, and in fairness to him we must say that it was about all he could do, was to make fun of piracy by occasionally writing about it. One of his earliest attacks was in *Hans Wursts Hochzeit*, completed some time before the end of 1774, where, as he said later in *Dichtung und Wahrheit*,[11] he could not resist poking fun at the notorious Macklot, who had his lair in Karlsruhe.[12] Not until 1779 do we hear from him anything more about pirates, although Himburg in Berlin had published unauthorized editions of Goethe's works in 1775, 1776, and 1779. But in 1779 Goethe sent to Charlotte von Stein a letter containing a poem written on the subject of Himburg. Many years later, in *Dichtung und Wahrheit,* he wrote an account of the episode, including the poem, although it is a revised version of the original. This is what he said: "Als nämlich meinen Arbeiten immer mehr nachgefragt, ja eine Sammlung derselben verlangt wurde, jene Gesinnungen[13] aber mich abhielten, eine solche selbst zu veranstalten, so benutzte Himburg mein Zaudern, und ich erhielt unerwartet einige Exemplare meiner zusammengedruckten Werke. Mit grosser Frechheit wusste sich dieser unberufene Verleger eines solchen dem Publikum erzeigten Dienstes gegen mich zu rühmen, und erbot sich, mir dagegen, wenn ich es verlangte etwas Berliner Porzellan zu senden. . . ."[14] But in spite of this he thought the Himburg edition of 1779 elegant enough to give away as a present to one of his feminine friends!

In 1781, in *Die Vögel,* there is a dialogue in which Hoffegut bemoans the misfortunes of authors, mentioning, among other things, the fact that their works are so often pirated.

There follows then a long silence on piracy except for his mention of it to Göschen, until in 1792 a letter which he wrote to Herder in July or August shows that he was again thinking about it. He was concerned about the possibility of the manuscript of the *Italienische Reise* falling into the hands of a pirate if he were to send it to friends to read. Here, after Goethe had had the Himburg experience, and after he has given piracy as one of the reasons for the publishing of the Göschen edition, one can say that he is openly opposing it.

Not until 1805 do we find mention of piracy again, in a letter to F. A. Wolf of February 25, in which Goethe said only that the pirates were much too busy. What is the explanation of this seeming lack of interest in one of the most widely discussed topics of the times? There may be two reasons. Goethe might have feared that any active participation on his part in an organized campaign against piracy would of necessity lead to all sorts of political complications. Then too he might have felt that although he was not a wealthy man he had sufficient income to live decently; hence the financial aspects of piracy did not loom large. His change of heart with regard to these financial aspects became extremely important when he fought successfully against piracy in 1822 and 1823.

In 1809, Goethe was apparently prepared to take a stand, presumably with Cotta, against the pirates, because on October 1 of that year he wrote that he had gone so far as to draw up a memorandum on the subject for public consumption. However, something (he referred to it as "ein Dämon") made him decide that this was not the time to involve himself in matters of public interest, and so he dropped the project. It would almost certainly have had political overtones, and he found this distasteful.

He thought that the Germans could not measure up to the rest of Europe in honesty and integrity where publishing was concerned. On November 9, 1810, Portalis, director of the royal press in France, informed him that a publisher in Cologne was preparing to issue an edition of *Die Wahlverwandtschaften* and inquired whether Goethe had given his permission. Goethe replied on November 25 that Cotta was the authorized publisher. In his *Tag- und Jahres-Hefte* for 1810, writing of this incident, he remarked: "So viel höher standen schon die Franzosen im Begriff von geistigen Besitz und gleichem Recht des Höhern und Niedern, wozu sich die guten Deutschen wohl sobald nicht erheben werden."[15]

Unlike Göschen, Cotta had apparently been unable to obtain Austrian privileges for his publication of Goethe's works. Hence it is hardly surprising that in 1810-11 an edition of twenty-six volumes appeared there entitled: *"Goethe's sämmt-liche Schriften.* Wien 1810 ff. Verlegt bey Anton Strauss. In Commission bey Geistinger." On November 16, 1810, Goethe asked Cotta if he could send him a copy of this edition. He spoke as though he knew something about the arrangement of the material and wished to find out what it contained over and above the Cotta edition, since he had thought of putting out a supplementary volume containing mainly miscellaneous poems. Apparently this plan came to naught, since there is no further discussion of the matter. In writing to Cotta, he showed little bitterness. He took this pirated edition quite calmly, and offered no suggestions as to how future depreda-tions might be discouraged. In the meantime, while he was displaying this unconcern about piracy, Cotta had become more and more irritated, and on March 7, 1812, wrote urgently, as we have seen, asking Goethe to make up his mind about put-ting out a cheaper edition as an answer to the Vienna one which, he had heard, was now being sold in Berlin.[16] Goethe's reply of March 17 was a masterly example of how to avoid giving a definite answer, and Cotta, knowing better than to begin a long and fruitless argument, dropped the topic of a cheap edition entirely.

However, this Viennese edition, plus the request from Cotta that he take action, seemed to make Goethe start think-ing more seriously of what was happening to his works. For the second time he decided to try to combat the pirates, but acting otherwise than in his previous attempt, he did not withdraw at the last minute. On the contrary, he made a defi-nite, if not strikingly original proposal. Writing to Cotta from Carlsbad on August 14, 1812, he said that according to in-formation he had received the only way to forestall piracy was to obtain a copyright in Austria. He then went on to suggest the publication of a new edition of the collected works. After agreement upon this plan, Cotta and Bertuch wished to start operations against the German pirates in Vienna, and so Ber-tuch asked Goethe for letters to various people of importance, including Metternich. On March 19, 1816, Cotta wrote Goethe to tell him that in order to avoid piracy of the new edition he would have to publish one in Austria.[17] Goethe agreed, but as we have seen, the consequences gave rise to a certain amount of unpleasantness between the two men.

The first indication that Goethe was considering some sort of action to safeguard himself and his heirs from the depredations of piratical publishers was a letter written to Friedrich von Müller on January 3, 1824, containing a request for a copy of a decision handed down by the king of Saxony on the subject of piracy. There is no record of any further activity on his part until November 2, when he sent a letter to Carl Ferdinand Friedrich von Nagler, the Prussian parliamentary representative.[18] The letter contains a series of rather flattering remarks. Goethe, who well knew how to approach those in authority, did not hesitate to appeal to any vanity in Nagler's make-up and, requesting complete secrecy, asked his support. In the enclosure to his letter Goethe informed Nagler of his intentions to publish a final and complete edition of his works, and impressed upon him the fact that piracy would naturally be a serious drawback to such an undertaking. He said that he knew that in the past individual rulers of various states had occasionally seen fit to grant sanctions to certain authors. Then came the all-important question:

> Würde daher ein Autor, der so viele Jahre in seinem Vaterlande gewirkt, dessen reine, mit allem bestehenden und zu wünschenden Guten im Einklang beharrende Thätigkeit dem Einsichtigen vor Augen liegt, einen allzukühnen Wunsch aussprechen, wenn er ein solches Privilegium von den verbündeten vereinigten Mächten sich erbäte und zwar für sich und die Seinigen, so dass er einen Selbstverlag unternehmen, oder wenn er einem Commissionair, vielleicht auch einem Verleger das Recht von seinen Geistesproducten merkantilischen Vortheil zu ziehen übertragen wollte, er auch zugleich auf diese den gesetzlichen Schutz zu erstrecken das Befugniss hätte?

(The somewhat casual reference to "a" publisher sounds cool and stand-offish, as though he was seriously considering a break with Cotta.)

Fortunately for Goethe, Nagler thought highly of him and consequently was willing to give him all possible assistance. On December 26 he wrote that he had on December 17 made an official representation of Goethe's request and had just received permission to support it in Vienna and the parliament. Nagler also sent Goethe a rough draft of an appeal to the parliament and advised him to write privately to Metternich and Gentz. (This parliament was the organ of the "Deutscher Bund," founded in 1815, which included thirty-four sovereign states and four free cities.) Wasting no time, Goethe wrote on January 7 to Gentz and on January 11 to Metternich requesting their intercession in his project. Again and again he emphasized "die Meinigen." He made very sure that his motives should not be misunderstood, and missed no opportunities to maintain good standing with all those who might possibly further his cause.

On January 11 Goethe wrote a formal petition: "An die deutsche Bundes-Versammlung," which is almost identical with the enclosure in the letter to Nagler of November 2, 1824. There was, however, a formal request which did not appear in the earlier letter. ". . . wage nunmehr nachstehende Bitte ehrerbietigst auszusprechen: Dass mir durch den Beschluss der hohen deutschen Bundes-Versammlung für die neue vollständige Ausgabe meiner Werke ein Privilegium ertheilt und dadurch der Schutz gegen Nachdruck in allen Bundesstaaten gesichert werde, unter Androhung der Confiscation und anderer Strafen, welche durch allgemeine gegen das Verbrechen des Nachdrucks künftig erfolgende Bundesbeschlüsse noch festgesetzt werden möchten. . . ."

In the letters from Nagler and Gentz which he received on January 29 Goethe heard that his petition was being looked upon with some favor in Vienna. The important part for him was that he wished to have a unanimous declaration from the general assembly granting him a copyright.

In all his dealings with the high-ranking statesmen of larger states, Goethe did not forget his own patron and ruler, Carl August, and on February 11 asked him if he would instruct his representative at the meeting to vote favorably for him. And on February 26 he requested Carl August to use his influence with other rulers on his behalf. It is not difficult to see how he marshaled all the forces at his command in order to obtain the prize which he felt was long overdue.

At this point, in order to clarify the situation, it will be well to separate the two sets of negotiations which were proceeding concurrently. For the moment we will confine ourselves to the progress of the efforts to obtain his copyright, and follow it to its conclusion.

Goethe's petition was first brought up for discussion in the parliament in the session of March 17, 1825.[19] The Prussian representative had hoped for a favorable decision immediately, but this was not to be the case. Some objections which were raised from the floor were not answered energetically enough by the chair (Austria), with the result that the petition was referred to the "Reklamations-Kommission" for review. On the basis of the report of this group the representatives of the parliament made the following recommendation: that since Goethe had addressed himself to the assembled delegates rather than to the state governments directly in order to avoid red tape, the delegates felt that they should recommend to their governments that the request be granted. This was going to involve just the kind of delay which Goethe wished to avoid.

In spite of the seeming unanimity among the assembled delegates, objections were raised in the session of March 24, although several members declared that they had already been authorized to support the petition. Whether Goethe was informed that his next step should be to write directly to the governments of states which were either hesitant or opposed to him, or whether he simply assumed that this was advisable cannot be stated with any certainty. But on March 28, after he had heard that the parliament had not immediately handed down a favorable decision, he wrote to von Fritsch, asking him for a list of the names and titles of all the delegates.

Just how much Goethe knew at this time of the complications attendant upon his petition is hard to say, but from the tone of his letters to friends one can infer that he was not entirely aware of the precariousness of his situation. As far as we know, Nagler did not inform him by letter how much opposition his plan had met, but according to Goethe's diary he had a visit from Nagler on March 29, so that Nagler must have told him of the complications which had arisen. In spite of the efforts of all those delegates who were favorably disposed towards Goethe, the opposition of two states was enough to prevent final action from being taken. Nagler had written the draft of a final decision and had presented it to his colleagues, but Bavaria and Württemberg declared that the parliament was not competent to pass upon such a matter and demanded that Goethe's request be refused without delay. His motives now came under suspicion, and it was even rumored that he had "gone over the head" of Carl August.

During these weeks, Goethe had had his troubles at home as well as in Frankfurt. On the night of March 21 the theater in Weimar burned to the ground. This event, added to the nervous strain of waiting for a decision from Frankfurt, affected him greatly, as we can see from his letters. He wrote to various friends, asking them not to visit him, since he was in no condition to see them, but on April 4, 1825, he was still sanguine about a speedy and favorable ruling from Frankfurt and expressed the hope that the government of Württemberg would see its way clear to come over to his side. He was showing remarkable self-restraint in the face of such unlooked-for delay. We have seen how irritated he would become if a publisher kept him waiting, but he had been in political circles long enough to realize that patience and tact would be his greatest allies at this time. There was no doubt that he was in a hurry, but he was determined not to injure his cause by any hasty steps which he might regret later on. He evidently realized that he could do nothing to avoid such complications. To protest would undoubtedly have had an adverse effect upon the parliament.

In the session of July 7, 1825, Nagler read a statement

to the assembled representatives. The gist of it was that Prussia was ready to grant Goethe's request and would issue a formal document as soon as the other states indicated their willingness to fall in line. The delegates of Bavaria and Württemberg then disclosed the information that their governments, upon receipt of a personal letter from Goethe, were prepared to grant his request, and said that he had already been apprised of this fact. Goethe, by this time a bit worried and irritated, wrote Graf Beust on July 22 that his last two letters to von Münch-Bellinghausen had gone unanswered. He enclosed with the letter those which he had composed for the governments of Saxony, Württemberg, and Bavaria, in accord with the information he had received about writing to them directly. Other problems had also arisen: Hessen wanted a definite statement as to the publisher; Württemberg wished to have the copyright statement printed in each volume of the edition. Goethe also wanted to know whether he should petition the Netherlands for the Luxembourg copyright.

In his letter to the three monarchs he said: "Sollte es hiebey nicht genehm seyn, diese Ausgabe der letzten Hand . . . auf unbestimmte Zeit zu privilegiren, so erlaube mir doch die allerunterthänigste Bitte, den anzusetzenden Termin auf fünfzig Jahre zu erstrecken. . . ." He was determined to find some sort of protection in these states which were not well disposed towards him, hence the alternate suggestion.

In spite of the drawn-out discussions and the hostility of some of the delegates of the parliament, half the battle had been won when, on August 23, 1825, Kaiser Franz I signed the document granting Goethe a copyright for the entire Austrian monarchy. Nagler, when the news reached him, must have been somewhat upset by the fact that his government had not yet taken the same action, particularly since he himself had been the strongest supporter of the petition.

On September 18, still mindful of the delay, Goethe wrote to Nagler, sending him a copy of Metternich's letter that contained the good news from Vienna and expressing the hope that Prussia would not delay much longer, since he was about to sign with Cotta. This he may have said in order to make his appeal more urgent, since he added that the contract depended upon complete protection against all piracy. Until December Nagler was apparently unable to accomplish much, but Goethe was not discouraged, particularly since he was receiving favorable replies from other states. Denmark was still uncertain, as we learn from a letter to Graf von Luxburg on October 1, and had indicated that it would grant a copyright only for fifty years. The state of Hessen limited the period to the years 1826-1835. The free cities were also doubtful.

Slowly but surely the copyright was spreading throughout German-speaking Europe. Goethe realized how slow progress was, but did not complain. Writing to Zelter on November 3, 1825, he said: "Die Verhandlungen wegen der neuen Ausgabe meiner Werke geben mir mehr als billig zu thun; sie sind nun ein ganzes Jahr im Gange; alles lässt sich aber so gut an und verspricht den Meinigen unerwartete Vortheile, um derentwillen es wohl der Mühe werth ist, sich zu bemühen." And we should remember that he had not only the negotiations for the copyright to attend to but in addition the supervision of the works for publication.

On November 25, in order to try to hasten the granting of privileges from Prussia, Goethe sent Nagler a copy of the Austrian document, asking that he be informed soon of the Prussian decision, favorable or otherwise.[20] On the 30th Nagler referred Goethe's letter to Bernstorff, who in turn communicated with von Schuckmann, Minister for the Interior. As a result of the wheels finally having been set in motion in high places, Friedrich Wilhelm III of Prussia affixed his signature to the copyright document on January 23, 1826.[21] Thus Goethe found himself in the enviable position of being the first German author to obtain for himself protection against piracy in almost all the German-speaking states of Europe. Only in Switzerland was the copyright not effective, and, as Cotta feared, a twelve-volume edition of his works was published in 1835 by the *Litterature-Comptoir* in Herisau.

We have followed this project of Goethe's through from conception to fulfillment. Putting his concurrent negotiations with Cotta to one side for a moment, we can say that as far as the copyright was concerned, his behavior was exemplary and even admirable. He pressed towards this goal with a single-ness of purpose and a tenacity which seems all the more re-markable when we consider his age. His desire to protect his family, along with a wish to see something concrete accom-plished to foil the pirate publishers, was the driving force.

III

From May 31, 1825, until March 12, 1826, Goethe had been far too occupied with the copyright problem to pay much at-tention to the preparations for publication of the *Ausgabe letzter Hand*. However, he had not let the whole matter drop, for we can see from a letter of March 12, 1826, to Göttling that he and his collaborators had made some progress with the revision and correction of his works.

He had nothing to say to Cotta until April 4, when he wrote to remind him that Cotta had once proposed a visit to Weimar to discuss details of the forthcoming publication. Cotta replied that the visit would have to be postponed, since he had two trips to make, to Munich and to Paris, which it was impossible to delay. He did, however, declare his willing-ness to carry out publication of a new edition in accordance with Goethe's every wish.

Goethe continued his own work and did not hesitate to send his friends more material for revision as they completed what they had previously received. But now, in addition to the procrastination of the assembly in Frankfurt, lack of activi-ty on Cotta's part began to plague Goethe. On May 2 he wrote to Sulpiz Boisserée, saying: "Buchhändlerische Aner-bieten von schöner Bedeutung habe schon mehrere. Freund Cottas Lauigkeit weiss mir nicht zu erklären; bemerken Sie, aber äussern Sie nichts." It is hardly surprising that as the time for the expiration of Cotta's rights drew near and no new agreement was made public, other publishing firms should begin to bid for the privilege of printing the new edition. On the other hand, in the light of what transpired later, Goethe may have been distorting the facts when he told Boisserée of having already received several attractive offers.

It is not necessary to discuss the beginning of Goethe's friendship with Boisserée, but the story of his services as intermediary between Goethe and Cotta is important for this study. It was actually not until later than the date of the letter quoted above that Goethe began to lean heavily on him. When financial negotiations began to run into difficulties, Goethe, with his dislike of personal bargaining, had Boisserée convey many of his proposals to Cotta.

Five days after his letter to Boisserée of May 2 Goethe received from Joseph Max, a bookdealer of Breslau, an offer of 30,000 taler for the rights to the new edition.[22] On May 10 he politely rejected the offer as not being adequate, but left the door open for further negotiations. He gave Max an idea of his plans for publication by saying that as soon as the copyright negotiations were successfully completed he would inform those bookdealers who were seriously interested of the scope and contents of the edition.

It is clear from this letter that Goethe now felt himself free to consider offers from other publishers. Although Cotta had the right to the first bid, Goethe was not bound to accept it, and the copyright which was now his placed him in a most advantageous bargaining position, whether he decided to continue his association with Cotta or not. Since no publisher could now make a low bid with the excuse that piracy would cut into his profits, Goethe could afford to be particular.

When Boisserée wrote next, on May 14, he had informed Cotta of these other offers. Cotta had shown great interest, saying that they would serve as a yardstick and that he was certain that he would be able to offer more than other publishers. On May 20 Goethe wrote to Cotta sending him the table of contents of the new edition and said that he would willingly allow him publishing rights over a period of twelve years. He then said that he had received some not inconsiderable offers and that he could not put off a decision much longer.[23] Therefore he wished Cotta to tell him immediately the amount "welche Sie mir und den Meinigen als den Schlussertrag meines ganzen schriftstellerischen Lebens zusagen können." His conscience may not have been quite at ease at the time, because he said there was no need for any personal interview. He wanted to avoid seeing Cotta, and possibly this was his way of hinting that he was displeased with the delay.

On May 20 he had also written to Boisserée, complaining that Cotta was very dilatory and saying that he had urged him to make an offer before departing for Paris. We can infer from this letter too that Goethe was considering the possibility of a break with Cotta quite seriously. However, we should bear in mind at the same time, since he told Boisserée to use what he had said to the best advantage, that he obviously expected his opinions to be passed on to Cotta. The hints about other publishers may have been simply weapons in a war of nerves, calculated to force Cotta to come to terms.

Boisserée, who by now was on excellent terms with Cotta, was able to reply to Goethe's letter of May 2 with information about the publisher's attitude. He had deemed it wise to mention casually to Cotta that Goethe had received offers from other publishers. Cotta replied that he would surely be able to offer more than anyone else, and on May 24 made the following proposal, which was typical of his methods: "Ich habe nach unserm letzten Vertrag bei gleichen Bedingungen den Vorzug vor allen andern Verlegern, ich könte mich daher blos darauf beschränken, zu erklären dass ich dem höchsten Gebot beitrette und dasselbige überneme—allein diss läge nicht in meiner Handlungsweise, die mich vielmehr veranlasst, zu erklären, dass ich mit Vergnügen 10,000 Thaler mehr als das höchste Gebot gewesen für die neue Ausgabe Ihrer Werke von 40 Bänden auf 12 Jahre bezahle." This was surely a most magnanimous gesture on Cotta's part. It should have immediately reassured Goethe that he was probably the only publisher in Germany to whom he could entrust the new edition with absolute confidence. But the stubborn old man now became greedy, influenced in part by his son, and put off his reply, hoping perhaps that a higher offer would be forthcoming.

In addition now to the two offers already received, a third was made by the publisher Georg Reimer of Berlin. He came to see Goethe in early July, but just what his proposal was we do not know.[24]

On July 30, Cotta, who had apparently been unable to make Goethe a definite offer prior to his Paris trip, wrote to complain that he had had no answer to his letter of May 24, either in Paris or in Stuttgart. The shade of Schiller arose before him, as he said: "Leider steht unser verewigter Freund, Schiller, uns nicht mehr zur Seite, der so freundlich und umsichtig das Finanzielle unserer Verhältnisse sonst besorgte. Sein Andenken und alles, was sich damit vereinigt und demselben in einem langen Zeitraum zart und schön anreiht, mag sich vertretten und wird gewiss im Stande seyn jedes Missverständniss zu heben wenn irgend eines derselben bestehen sollte."[25] Goethe's answer of August 5 showed a certain relief at the idea of an intermediary, and he immediately suggested that Boisserée assume the responsibility. He then wrote on August 19 to Boisserée, giving him all the information necessary for his role. Boisserée was the last, and with the possible exception of Schiller, the most important of all the mediators upon whom Goethe relied so heavily in negotiating with his publishers. It will perhaps be worth while to digress from our study of Goethe's relations with Cotta to discuss this peculiar dependence upon a third person.

IV

We can trace this distaste of dealing directly with a publisher to his indoctrination by Behrisch in Leipzig; we may remind ourselves of the first time that a publisher, Fleischer, rejected Goethe's offer of a manuscript. We may say then that as a result of this episode it was not unnatural that Goethe looked upon an open refusal as an affront. What is more, he had an aversion to financial dickering, which he considered beneath his dignity. Perhaps an explanation of his use of intermediaries and at the same time a reflection on the character of publishers in general is his picture of Mittler in *Die Wahlverwandtschaften*. This well-meaning individual, whose name is his profession, is usually successful in his efforts only when concerned with persons of average and lower than average intellect and sensibility.

Goethe's literary activities prove that it was well-nigh impossible for him to get along without a mediator between him and his publishers. And yet, in his youth at least, he was apparently not averse to dealing directly with them—provided it was not his work for which he was negotiating. This is best illustrated by his services as mediator for Lavater and also for Salzmann. There are occasional instances in later years of his assuming the same role. His introduction of Boisserée and Eckermann to Cotta is a case in point.

In looking for the first instance of Goethe's use of an intermediary, we must turn to Merck. It was he who succeeded in removing the barrier which Behrisch had set up between Goethe and the publication of his work. By persuading Goethe that the two of them should publish *Götz,* he broke down Goethe's early inhibitions. And it was Merck who, in 1776, insisted that *Stella* be published and who approached Mylius about it.

With editors and publishers whom he knew personally, the young Goethe was on more cordial terms. As a result we know of no one acting as mediator for Jacobi's publication of *Erwin und Elmire* in the *Iris* in 1775, nor for Weygand's publication of *Werther*. However, it is possible that if, as we suspect, Goethe was in need of money, he swallowed his pride and offered Jacobi the manuscript directly.

When Bertuch came forward and offered his services as mediator with Göschen, Goethe accepted gladly. He realized, in a vague sort of way, that for the first time in his life he was to become involved in a publishing venture of large scope. He had had no experience in such matters, nor did he know of a publisher who would be willing to undertake the task. What he did know, however, was that he did not trust publishers, and that he was not going to approach one directly. From this time onward, he never entered into any important contractual agreement with a publisher without depending upon a third person to negotiate for him. Once the preliminary chores had been completed, he often carried on a lively and sometimes heated correspondence with his publisher.

We may pass over the services of the mediators in the cases of Unger and Vieweg rather briefly. Moritz and Bertuch did little more for Goethe than introduce him to Unger. Since no formal contract existed between author and publisher in this instance, Goethe was not much concerned about what might happen, and as we have seen, he soon discovered that he had Unger completely under his thumb. Böttiger's role as intermediary for Vieweg is not quite clear, and since there were no real negotiations but a sovereign demand from Goethe and immediate acquiescence on Vieweg's part, no more need be said on the subject.

The pattern of Goethe's procedure in dealing with his publishers by means of a third person is now fairly well established, but it is interesting to note that with the exception of Böttiger, none of the mediators upon whom Goethe relied were what one could call completely disinterested persons. Merck was an intimate friend as well as a business partner. Bertuch was certainly interested, since he had put up part of the capital with which Göschen was to work. Böttiger, as far as we know, stood to gain nothing by his mediation for Vieweg, nor was he a particular friend of Goethe's. Probably he felt that it was easier to comply with Goethe's request than to refuse. When we come to Schiller, we find that his case is again different from those which preceded it. Schiller found himself in what must have been a peculiar and ticklish situation. His friendship and admiration for Goethe are axiomatic, but at the same time he entertained almost as great a friendship and respect for Cotta. This immediately becomes evident upon reading the correspondence between them. Many of the letters show the formal, businesslike relationship which is a part of any author's association with his publisher, but there are just as many revealing the deeper feelings which each had for the other. Vollmer, the editor of the Schiller-Cotta correspondence, speaks of the "Freundschaftsverhaltnis . . . dessengleichen fast kein zweites zwischen Dichter und Verleger zu finden sein dürfte."[26]

The fact that Schiller was so close to both men must have made his task very difficult, but there is no indication that he ever balked or even complained. What made his position awkward was that he had to try to keep faith with both sides. Like Boisserée after him, he smoothed over many of Goethe's rather blunt remarks before communicating them to Cotta, and did the publisher a service by telling him what he thought of Goethe as an author and as a businessman. It appears from his correspondence that he was rather more frank and informative with Cotta than with Goethe. However, we should recall that for him personal contact with Goethe was possible, so that he could have said much about Cotta directly. But his allegiance was obviously divided, and to his credit he handled the whole affair successfully. On more than one occasion after his death both Goethe and Cotta expressed regret over the fact that he was no longer available as mediator.

Schiller's mediation began as soon as he had obtained Goethe's assurance of his participation in the *Horen,* since Cotta was the publisher and controlled the pursestrings. In order not to antagonize Goethe, Schiller was most careful to handle him as tactfully as possible, and he naturally wished Cotta to do the same. Thus he had to inform Cotta of many of Goethe's idiosyncrasies. For instance, at the beginning of Goethe's association with the *Horen,* Schiller sent a plea to Cotta, writing on November 14, 1794, as follows: "Vor allen Dingen aber bitte und beschwöre ich Sie, für eine genaue Correctur zu sorgen. . . . Einige unsrer Mitglieder, z. B. Göthe, sind in Diesem Stück äusserst empfindlich und wir könnten sie verlieren, wenn sie hierin Ursache zur Unzufriedenheit bekämen." Trying to keep the peace all round, he told

Cotta so much about Goethe that the publisher was probably not greatly surprised at some of his later demands. Schiller also made all sorts of suggestions as to how they could be sure of keeping him as a contributor and collaborator. He was a far more ingenious businessman than Goethe, thinking up little schemes which the latter would never have dreamed of. For instance, knowing Cotta's generosity and business acumen, he wrote to him on December 22, 1794, saying that it would be a good idea if Cotta added something to Goethe's next honorarium. Goethe would thus be obligated and it would be money well spent, because he would then send Cotta more material and would not ask so much for it. Even in the short period during which he had been associated with Goethe he had come to know him better than most people, because Goethe, recognizing a kindred spirit, had been more frank and communicative with him than with others. Thus Schiller could tell Cotta in the same letter, with reference to the above plan: "Diess ist, wie gesagt, bloss bey Göthen nöthig, der zwar nicht eigennützig ist, aber doch erwartet, dass er bey den Horen besser als sonst irgendwo bezahlt wird."

His enthusiasm for Goethe, as illustrated by his constant reiteration that he must be retained as contributor, transmitted itself to Cotta after his first meeting with Goethe in 1797. From then on we find Cotta frequently asking Schiller to make sure that Goethe was well disposed towards him. He was obviously anticipating the day when he and Goethe would be working together, and Schiller did not disappoint him.[27] In addition to wishing to see two of his greatest friends conclude an agreement which would be of inestimable benefit to both of them he may well have foreseen that such an association would add immeasurably to the prestige of German letters. Cotta was only too anxious to enter into a business relationship with Goethe, but Schiller knew that the latter was wary of publishers, and he worked hard to swing everything in Cotta's favor.

Schiller's usually astute judgment in acting as go-between was once clouded by his admiration for Goethe when he urged

Cotta on May 29 to take up the publication of the *Propyläen,*
saying that a periodical which Goethe edited was bound to be
a success and bring new glory to the house of Cotta. Cotta
unfortunately lost a considerable sum in this undertaking. To
his credit, however, this loss did not deter him from continuing his relationship with Goethe. Schiller never gave up hope
that Goethe would finish *Faust,* and never ceased to communicate that hope to Cotta, reminding him on December 16
that Goethe would want "ein derbes Honorar." On March 24,
1800, he wrote Cotta that Goethe would need a very attractive
offer if he were to finish *Faust.* He said further: "Er rechnet
freilich auf einen grossen Profit, weil er weist, dass man in
Deutschland auf dieses Werk sehr gespannt ist. Sie können
ihn, dass bin ich überzeugt, durch glänzende Anerbietungen
dahin bringen, dieses Werk in diesem Sommer auszuarbeiten.
. . . Er fodert nicht gern und lässt sich lieber Vorschläge thun,
auch accordiert er lieber ins Ganze als Bogenweis."

Schiller's letter to Cotta on May 18 gave an interesting
picture of Goethe the businessman. He referred to Goethe's
stipulations for the publication of the *Taschenbuch auf das
Jahr 1804,* and added:

Vielleicht könnten Sie aber alle diese Risikos nicht achten, in der
Hoffnung, sich auf einmal an dem *Goethischen Faust* für alle
Verluste zu entschädigen. Aber ausserdem, dass es zweifelhaft
ist, ob er dieses Gedicht je vollendet, so können Sie sich darauf
verlassen, dass er es Ihnen, der vorgehenden Verhältnisse und
von Ihnen aufgeopferten Summen ungeachtet, nicht wohlfeiler
verkaufen wird, als irgend einem anderen Verleger, und seine
Forderungen werden gross sein. Es ist, um es gerade heraus zu
sagen, kein guter Handel mit G. zu treffen, weil er seinen Wert
ganz kennt und sich selbst hoch taxiert, und auf das Glück des
Buchhandels, davon er überhaupt nur eine vage Idee hat, keine
Rücksicht nimmt. Es ist noch kein Buchhändler in Verbindung
mit ihm geblieben und mancher mochte auch mit ihm nicht
zufrieden sein. Liberalität gegen seine Verleger ist seine Sache
nicht.

Whether Cotta took these words of Schiller to heart is not

known, but he was not at all discouraged by this rather unprepossessing picture. The *Cellini* was finally accepted after Schiller had told Cotta on October 24 that he ought to make Goethe set his figure and then Cotta would be in a position to bargain.[28] This, of course, was one of the reasons for Goethe's dislike of naming his own figure. He much preferred the publisher to make an offer, so that he could then accept or reject it.

Schiller's services as mediator reached their peak on October 16, 1804, when he informed Cotta that Goethe was seriously considering publication of a new edition of his collected works. He wrote that Goethe had told him his terms, in part, and he advised Cotta to ask for something specific which he could publish. This, he felt, would bring Goethe to the point where he would offer Cotta the new edition. Cotta expressed himself as willing to undertake the venture, with certain reservations, but unfortunately Goethe hesitated so long in making up his mind that this proved to be the last time that Schiller could act as a buffer between them.

We may now say that there was hardly a single publication of one of Goethe's works from 1797 to 1804 for which Schiller did not play the part of mediator. After Schiller's death, Goethe found himself without anyone to whom he felt he could entrust such a delicate task. He was fully aware of the burden which Schiller had lifted from his shoulders, as is apparent from a letter to Cotta written on May 10, 1812: "Wie sehr hätte ich seit dem siebzehnten vorigen Monats gewünscht dass der edle Schiller noch leben möchte; er war bey unsern Angelegenheiten ein so lieber als glücklicher Mittelsmann. Was mich betrifft; so fühl ich immer aufs neue wie peinlich es ist mit Personen, mit denen man nur in sittlichem Verhältniss zu stehen wünscht, über öconomische Gegenstände zu handeln."[29]

Besides an expression of regret, this letter contains the first real explanation as to why Goethe preferred not to deal directly with publishers. But we should be careful not to apply this statement to every publisher with whom he negotiated.

Of all those with whom he was associated, there were probably only two, Cotta and Frommann, with whom we can imagine his becoming friendly, so that his statement explains only a small part of his feelings on the subject.

In addition to what Goethe himself gives us as a reason for his desire—one might even say need—to have someone else act for him with his publishers, we may advance a theory which is perhaps valid in a more general sense. Ever since about 1797 he had become more and more convinced that he was a genius who stood far above his fellow-men. Why, then, should he subject himself to dealing with publishers, of whom he had entertained a low opinion long before that time? He had made up his mind that they were individuals whom he could not trust, and as a result felt that he could not and should not be expected to descend to their level and waste valuable time bickering and haggling. His mission was to create his works, and once he had decided that the public was to receive the benefit of them, it was up to someone else to attend to the unpleasant details of how and when they were to be published. Unfortunately this distrust of the publishing guild often forced him against his will into the many painful controversies in which he became involved. But in so far as it was possible for him, he was not going to sully himself by acting like a merchant. Someone may counter by saying that after all he did do the bargaining, since he laid down the terms for the mediator to transmit to the publisher. This is quite true, but his attempt to avoid direct contact with this inferior individual was enough to satisfy his ego and helped assure him that he was not losing his self-respect.

V

By now it is evident that one of Goethe's main concerns over the final edition of his works was the realization that his writing was all that he could leave his family. So it is hardly surprising to find him telling Boisserée on August 13, 1825, that he was leaving his literary work to his son as capital. No wonder, he went on, that August valued the results of his life more highly than he himself had ever done.[30]

In a long supplement to this letter he proceeded to reveal to his friend the situation as it was. In order to be able to devote more time to the supervision of the preparations for the edition, he had handed over all "technische, ökonomische und merkantilische Behandlung" to his son. August had then conferred with his associates as to the best method of procedure. All sorts of suggestions had been made: that Goethe should publish the edition himself, that a society should be formed to handle it, that he should receive royalties, and other similar propositions. As much as 50,000 taler, with the probability of more, had been offered, so that Cotta would have to pay between 60,000 and 70,000 in line with his previous bid. But August and his advisers thought that it would be possible to obtain at least 100,000 taler.[31] Boisserée by now must have realized that Goethe was being influenced to no small extent by August and his drinking companions. Moreover, he must have thought it strange that Goethe did not tell him who had offered 50,000 taler. After all, if Boisserée was now the principal link between Goethe and Cotta, he should have been entitled to all the information which Goethe had in his possession. Returning to the subject of his relationship with Cotta, Goethe continued that since Cotta was better equipped than anyone else to undertake the task, he wished he would stop vacillating, which was especially awkward for Goethe in his old age. He wanted Cotta as his publisher, he claimed, and was most anxious to see matters cleared up while he himself was still alive. Boisserée transmitted this information to Cotta in his usual tactful fashion, and the publisher then wrote to Goethe from Cologne on August 27.[32] He told him that by his offer of 10,000 taler more than the highest bidder, he had intended to prove that their relationship was not based merely upon a contract, but that he valued it above all else. He felt, however, that August's suggestion of 100,000 taler was realistic only if one could be assured of a very enthusiastic reception by the public. For his part, he offered another plan. He suggested a method of payment which would vary proportionately with the sale of the edition. Sixty thousand taler, in line with his offer of 10,000 more than the bid of 50,000 which had been made, would stand as his payment under any circumstances. Then he would be willing to add to that 20,000 taler for every 10,000 subscribers over and above 20,000. Hence, if 30,000 persons subscribed, Goethe's remuneration would be 80,000 taler and so on. He concluded his letter by saying that this meant that the fee would increase proportionately to the public interest, without, however, being entirely dependent upon it. The price of the edition, he went on, would have to be very reasonable in order to attract the maximum number of subscribers. By all standards this was a sensible proposition —far more so than August's wild demand for 100,000 taler outright. But Goethe, who was haggling now as he had never felt it necessary to do before, did not accept immediately. However, on September 11 he wrote to Gentz asking again if he could possibly speed up the granting of the Austrian sanction, so that he could use it in order to try to obtain the unanimous decision of the parliament. He gave as the reason for the urgency of his appeal the fact that he was about to sign a contract with Cotta, a contract which would need for its basis the copyright for the German-speaking part of Europe.[33]

If Goethe really meant what he said about being almost ready to sign with Cotta, credit must be given in large measure to Boisserée, who had told him more than once that he would be better off to accept an offer from a publisher than to publish the edition on his own.[34] It seems quite likely that once Goethe had handed over the task of mediation to Boisserée, he probably had every intention of signing with Cotta, but the prolonged negotiations were due partly to external pressure, partly to his desire to drive as hard a bargain as possible with his publisher. Boisserée's strong recommendation that Cotta's plan be accepted eventually made Goethe decide to remain with him. The whole picture, however, becomes somewhat confusing because of the fact that not until March 1826 was a final contract signed. But Goethe must have arrived at a decision shortly before September 24, 1825, on which date he wrote to Boisserée to say how pleased he was to be able to celebrate at one and the same time the restoration of a relationship which was so dear to him and the conclusion of such important affairs. Two days later, August von Goethe, writing for his father, told Cotta that he was happy that a relationship which his father had enjoyed for so long was to be extended to himself and his family.[35] Enclosed in the letter were also three supplementary documents, one of which was the preliminary draft of a contract.

While the Prussian copyright and others from minor states were hanging fire, Cotta agreed to all thirteen points which had been laid down in this rough draft. And then, in spite of the fact that Goethe had seemingly made up his mind, for some reason he began haggling and hesitating all over again. On November 20, after raising several questions which had occurred to him and his son, the point was again brought up that he had received and was still receiving interesting bids from other publishers.[36] Almost certainly he reopened this topic at the insistence of his son. He impressed upon Cotta again that a final decision should be reached, claiming that he simply did not know which way to turn in the face of so many attractive offers.

What Cotta said in his reply of November 30 we do not know, but an answer, signed jointly by Goethe and August on December 21, discussed once more the possibility of a payment of 100,000 taler. Thus the whole process of negotiation seemed to have returned to the point from whence it started. Cotta was told that all the evidence pointed to a sale of 40,000 copies. In addition to demanding a flat sum of 100,000 taler, Goethe wished to accept Cotta's offer of increased payment proportionate to the number of copies sold. He also wanted to have two editions, one in large format, the other smaller.

Boisserée, having seen Goethe's previous demand for 100,000 taler, did his best to dissuade him from insisting upon such an enormous sum. On December 28 he wrote saying that in his opinion Goethe's family could rest assured with the plans already made. Of course, higher offers should not be summarily rejected, but Goethe should be very cautious about the ability of other publishers to pay these large fees. Some impartial observers, said Boisserée, were even concerned over the risk Cotta was taking in offering so much.[37] We can be very sure that the observers whose opinions he referred to in this letter were far more reliable than the "advisers" with whom August was wont to associate.

In the days following this letter, Boisserée spent much of his time discussing with Cotta Goethe's demands and the implications of his renewed negotiations for higher payment.[38] He told Goethe that Cotta was quite hurt by his letter, not only because the latter had thought—with good reason—that everything had been settled, but also because Goethe was showing evidence of distrust by not revealing the other offers. Cotta could not possibly commit himself more than he had already, for in spite of the privileges already granted, there was still the possibility of piracy in Switzerland, Alsace, and the Netherlands. Another reason, and one which shows just how great a risk he was taking by making his extraordinarily generous offer, was that he still had remainders from the previous Goethe edition which were gathering dust on his shelves. Boisserée continued by saying that if Goethe and his son did not wish to continue this association, Cotta would not be able to give up his rights to many of Goethe's individual works, because this would bring hardship on him and his family. This was the first time that Cotta had sent anything approaching an ultimatum to Goethe, and the mention of his family may have been a gentle reminder that he too had children for whom he wished to provide. If, Boisserée went on to say, neither side could agree to relax its conditions, then of course Goethe would have to take his business elsewhere. In any case, Cotta should be informed as to the amounts of other offers received and their sources—information to which he was entitled.

Goethe's respect for his friend's good judgment, and perhaps a secret feeling that Cotta was right after all, turned the tide once more in Cotta's favor—with reservations, for Goethe was not yet prepared to give in once and for all. On January 8, 1826, he told Boisserée that in view of his recommendations he would take up Cotta's offer once more, albeit unwillingly, and only under the condition that he also profit in some other manner. He therefore again enclosed the draft of a contract.

However, he was still not completely mollified and continued to distrust Cotta and his motives. There is perhaps some excuse for his attitude, but one might think that he would have been able, once the matter was settled, to forget past grievances and to co-operate with his publisher as best he could. After all, he was the one who stood to gain most by this new edition, not Cotta. But on January 12 he explained his dissatisfaction to Boisserée as follows:

> Lassen Sie mich jedoch das Hauptübel, das bey dieser Verhandlung obwaltet, aussprechen: es ist diess: dass der Verleger jederzeit genau weiss was ihm und seiner Familie frommt, der Autor dagegen völlig darüber im Dunkeln ist. Denn wo sollte er in dem völlig gesetzlosen Zustande des deutschen Buchhandels Kenntniss nehmen was darinnen Rechtens ist, was Herkommens und was noch sonstiger Convenienz Buchhändler sich einander verzeihen und gegen die Autoren erlauben. Daher kommt es bald dass der Verleger sich gar bald, auch in den wichtigsten Fällen, entschliesst, der Autor dagegen schwanken und zaudern muss.

Referring to publishing and publishers in general, these words might be justified, but Goethe apparently did not recall that Cotta had suffered substantial losses for his sake on the *Propyläen,* that he had made little if any profit on *Dichtung und Wahrheit* or the scientific works, and that copies of the previous edition of Goethe's collected works had accumulated in the warehouse in Stuttgart. However, even Goethe seemed to be tiring of the constant sequence of proposal and counterproposal, and he informed Boisserée that he would now let bygones be bygones, but in answer to the suggestion that Cotta should be informed about the offers from other publishers, all Goethe would say was that since April of 1825 he had received twenty bids from other quarters, the three latest being one of 70,000 and two of 80,000 taler.[39]

Nor was Boisserée's task ended yet. In closing the letter Goethe begged him to continue his good work, since he anticipated that there would still be misunderstandings and conflicts which Boisserée could smooth out. Boisserée transmitted the terms to Cotta, who agreed: 1) to publish the edition; 2) to pay 60,000 taler for forty volumes and to pay for any further volumes on a corresponding scale, with the stipulation that he be free to publish all individual works from then on; 3) to pay a special fee for the octavo edition, in case the regular edition sold 20,000 copies. Boisserée assured Goethe that Cotta realized perfectly how much concerned he was over his family, and said that he thought Goethe would be entirely satisfied with Cotta's offer. Again he urged Goethe to make known to Cotta the amounts of the various offers, saying that Cotta was expecting this move. In a more personal letter, written two days later on January 23,[40] he told Goethe how upset he was at what the latter had said about the status of the author with regard to his publisher. It is almost touching to see the interest Boisserée was taking in his task of mediation. Being as fond of both men as he was, his efforts to bring the affair to a successful conclusion were prodigious, and his tact and skilful handling show that he was a friend and diplomat of the highest order. His greatest asset was that he knew Cotta far better than Goethe did, and to Goethe's credit he eventually admitted this by his acceptance of what Boisserée had to say about Cotta's intentions and his character.

Boisserée tried to impress upon Goethe that Cotta had done his utmost, assuring him that the publisher had already sacrificed hopes of a substantial profit, and that he was sure Goethe could take Cotta's word for it.[41] He urged Goethe therefore to come to terms immediately, mentioning yet another reason: Cotta, in spite of his desire to secure for himself the rights to the new edition, was finally becoming impatient. Boisserée went on to say that if Goethe did not accept Cotta's latest terms, the publisher would be forced to revert to his original offer of 10,000 taler more than the highest bidder, and would have to insist upon the stipulations of the previous contract.[42] He pleaded with Goethe to place his complete trust in Cotta. Goethe, grateful to Boisserée, and apparently tired of the prolonged arguments and negotiations, answered on January 30, 1826, with the following brief note: "Euer Wort sey ja! ja! also ja! und Amen!! Das nähere nächstens."[43]

One is tempted to say that Goethe was hypocritical in his dealings with Cotta during these years. Of course, he said to Boisserée what he would never have said to Cotta, knowing that the former would transmit the gist of his remarks in his usual diplomatic fashion. But when he wrote directly to his publisher, he was often most polite and flattering, acting as though there had never been any question about the publication of his works by Cotta. Such a letter was the one of February 3, 1826, in which he assured Cotta that for the first time in years he felt "eine wahrhafte Zufriedenheit . . . wo ich gewiss bin dass die Resultate meiner literarischen Thätigkeit in Ihre Hände gelegt sind; ein gültigeres Zeugniss wechselseitigen Vertrauens konnte nicht gegeben werden." The publisher's reaction was one of gratitude and relief.

Euer Excellenz weiss ich mich in Worten nicht auszudrücken, wie mich das frühere Schreiben an Freund Boisserée und das an mich vom 3. dieses Monats ergriffen und gerührt hat. Woran ich nie zweifeln konnte, hat sich dadurch bewahrt: Ihr hoher, schöner Sinn hat auch hier das Rechte ergriffen, was in diesem delikaten Verhältnisse uns allen wahrhafte Zufriedenheit gewähren kann. Den innigsten herzlichsten Dank dafür. Mein tief betrübtes und bewegtes Gemüt hat sich dadurch wieder gehoben und so wie ich nun wieder mit Freude und Lust an dieses Geschäft gehe, so wird es auch mein ganzes Bemühen sein, es mit Würde und zu beiderseitiger Ehre und Vorteil zu betreiben.

However, when Goethe eventually answered Cotta's request to see the other offers which had been made, he again refused, on the grounds that he would be breaking faith with those who had made them. As if to impress upon both Boisserée and Cotta that he was doing the latter a great favor, he emphasized how he had only recently rejected a substantial sum from a reliable firm. It is difficult to advance reasons, other than Goethe's, as to why he objected so strongly to divulging such information to Cotta. There are two possible answers for his being so reticent about the whole matter. One is that he based his reasoning on an exaggerated sense of honor. Another and more likely explanation is that he was enjoying himself. The copyright was now his, and it and the other offers made a weapon which he could use to keep Cotta at bay.

On April 16, 1826, Goethe had been able to send Cotta the first five volumes of his revised and corrected works. He brought to Cotta's attention the fact that he had made certain orthographical changes, principally the correction of *ss* to *sz,* and *y* to *i.* (He himself did not adhere to these changes in his personal correspondence.) As usual, he impressed upon the publisher the need for care and accuracy, although he omitted the usual harangue on the subject of misprints.

One of the first points to which Goethe turned his attention was the physical aspect of the forthcoming edition. Having received assurances from Cotta that all possible care would be taken to eliminate typographical errors, he himself wrote on May 26 to Albrecht Le Bret, who, along with Cotta's man Reichel, was going to supervise the printing, telling him that careful work would be profitable in the long run, since a prospective buyer would react favorably to a finished piece of work. In a letter to Cotta of May 28 he declared himself well satisfied with the appearance of samples of paper and printing. Two factors were obviously controlling his interest here: first, that this was the last edition of his works which he would see and he wished it to be as attractive as possible, and second, that a relatively cheap edition which looked reasonably attractive would sell.

It was, however, impossible for Goethe to be satisfied with his publisher for any length of time, and so on August 9 he was politely but firmly prodding Cotta to send him the proposed copies of the public announcement of the new publication. To Boisserée he was more outspoken on the subject and called Cotta's behavior "etwas bedenklich." He was determined, however, that the delay should not work to his disadvantage, and insisted on September 30 that Cotta prolong the subscription period. Any changes which Cotta thought it necessary to make concerning the subscription would have to be made public, together with the statement that they were being made with Goethe's consent.

Goethe seemed to be determined to think that the whole venture of the new edition was a conspiracy of which he was the intended victim. The strain of such an attitude must have been extraordinarily hard on him, since he must have feared that every letter from Cotta contained some subtle scheme which would harm him and his family. And as if his self-torture over Cotta were not enough, outside dangers made their appearance, as, for instance, when Grillparzer told him that he had seen in Vienna an advertisement of the new edition published by a bookseller by arrangement with Cotta's firm.[44] Although he protested to Boisserée on October 17 that he would never have entertained the idea that Cotta could have drawn a third person into the venture behind his back, he nevertheless wanted a check made. Fortunately, there was nothing to the story.

The next point which served to increase the tension was a request by Cotta on October 11 to change the order of publication of certain volumes of the regular edition.[45] He thought that since he was so pressed for time it would be advisable to have two volumes of the second installment replacing two of the first. The contract stated that the edition was to be completed within four years, with two installments of five volumes each appearing annually. Cotta was apparently having difficulty in preparing the volumes of poems and suggested that two volumes of prose be inserted into the first installment instead. Goethe told Boisserée to inform Cotta in no uncertain terms that such a change was not to take place, since complaints had been made about similar changes in the publication of Schiller's works. Moreover, he thought that such an alteration would be a breach of faith with the public. Then, too, his anxiety to impress upon his readers that there really was something different about this edition made it imperative that the Helena scenes of *Faust* be included in the fifth volume, the last of the first installment. We can interpret this to mean that he wished the public to look forward anxiously to each fresh installment as a result of having found something new and unexpected in the earlier volumes.

For a period of several months now everything seemed to move along according to plan. The proofs of the new edition were appearing, and Goethe was satisfied with them. However, as the weeks passed and the work accumulated, Goethe found himself hard put to maintain his original enthusiasm. Writing to Nees von Esenbeck on April 4, 1827, he said: "Ein solches Unternehmen in Gang zu bringen gibt so viel Beschäftigung, dass es einem fast reuen möchte es unternommen zu haben." Then he was worried for fear that there should be errors in the revision which could not be corrected in time, but he consoled himself with the comforting thought that, after all, people had been correcting the classics for several thousand years.

Cotta was having his difficulties as well, since certain volumes of the edition were proving to be too large and too expensive to print as Goethe wished. He asked permission to omit some material from them, to be included elsewhere. He admitted that the fault lay with him, since he had calculated 107-110 sheets for each installment of the edition, and found now that the second had run to 141. He was rather annoyed by the fact that at the date of writing, July 6, he had received no answer to his letter of April 12.[46] In that letter he explained that he had seen, in the sixth issue of *Über Kunst und Alterthum,* the announcement of the first installment of the *Ausgabe letzter Hand.* It contained the remark: ". . . dass hier ein lebender Autor selbst . . . möglichste Sorge getragen." Cotta took this to be a slighting reference on Goethe's part to the posthumous Schiller edition which had met with so little enthusiasm, and was deeply hurt. He wrote to Goethe about it, trying to explain why the Schiller edition had turned out so badly, but received no reply. Goethe replied to Cotta's letter of July 6 on the 26th, agreeing to the proposed changes, but making no reference to Cotta's letter of April 12.

Cotta wrote again on October 9, referring to his unanswered letter. He had been so hurt, he said, by Goethe's complete indifference to his sincere remarks that he wished to have the letter returned. This made sufficient impression upon Goethe for him to write on October 24, 1827, what is almost an apology. It was not in keeping with his character that he should apologize, and he did not go quite that far, but it was a conciliatory letter, and he seemed anxious to reassure Cotta of his good will. He had long been convinced, he said, that the shortcomings of the Schiller edition were due to unfavorable circumstances rather than to any neglect on Cotta's part. He concluded by agreeing to the changed arrangement of material, saying that the public would be surprised by something unexpected, and he would see to it that the third group of volumes to be published also contained similar material.

Excepting the unpleasantness over the publication of the Goethe-Schiller correspondence, the relationship between Goethe and Cotta continued in a fairly satisfactory manner. The only other drawback to the publication of the new edition was Goethe's difficulty in filling out the three volumes containing *Wilhelm Meisters Wanderjahre*. We have seen elsewhere how worried he became over the fact that the public would feel it was not getting its money's worth in these slender volumes, and there is something admirable but at the same time pathetic in the sight of the old man desperately trying to find sufficient material.[47]

As far back as June 11, 1823, Goethe had hinted to his publisher that he was intending to make public his correspondence with Schiller from the years 1794 to 1805. However, since he was so occupied otherwise, it was not until May of the following year that we find mention of this plan again. In the meantime, negotiations had been taking place between

Cotta and the Schiller family and between Goethe and the Schiller family. Wilhelm von Humboldt, as we hear in a letter of March 26, 1824, from Charlotte Schiller to Cotta,[48] also had a hand in the negotiations, although to what extent it is difficult to say.[49] Charlotte sent Cotta the agreement she had reached with Goethe, written by him.[50] From what she said, the main point was that the payment was to be divided equally between Goethe and Schiller's family.[51] If Cotta agreed to the terms, she was prepared to send to Goethe letters which he had written to Schiller. This she did in April 1824[52] and Cotta promised to carry on further negotiations with Goethe. The first letter which Cotta sent is not available to us, but Goethe's reply of May 30 indicated that he was still too busy to be able to make any decision. However, in the autumn of 1824 he told Caroline von Wolzogen that the manuscript would be ready by the following Easter and that Cotta was going to have to pay more than he had anticipated.

On July 10, 1825, Goethe wrote to Caroline to say that he would be in a position to pay 2,000 taler (half of the Schiller family's share of the honorarium) by Michaelmas. Sometime between October and December Ernst von Schiller wrote Caroline Schiller that Goethe had not yet paid and in March of the following year he reminded Goethe of this.[53] August von Goethe, replying for his father, claimed that they had no recollection of such an agreement, and on July 31 Ernst, highly incensed, wrote to his brother Carl that he would not hesitate to hale Goethe into court if he delayed any longer. "Denn es ist abscheulich," he wrote, "dass Goethe, der Freund, d. h. der angebliche Freund unseres Vaters, dass Goethe, der Minister und nun reiche Mann, erschlichene Vorteile gegen die es bedürfenden Hinterbliebenen seines Freundes benutzt und Verbindlichkeiten zu erfüllen von sich ablehnt, die auch der Bettler, wenn er redlich ist, nach Kräften zu erfüllen sich bestrebt. Die Sache ist so schreiend, dass ich glaube, Goethe wird sich schämen und zahlen."[54] Between the date of this letter and September matters were apparently settled, since on September 20 Ernst formally gave his agreement to the rough draft of the contract between Goethe and Cotta. The manuscript was now ready for the printer.

By January 26, 1827, documents dealing with the negotiations for publication had gone to Stuttgart, while the manuscript was still in Goethe's possession. In October Cotta was most anxious to begin printing, but Goethe was still so concerned about his motives that he refused to send the manuscript unless Cotta paid him cash on delivery.[55] This is to all intents and purposes what he meant when he wrote to Cotta on December 17 that since the publisher had not yet committed himself to the stipulations of the rough draft of the contract he could not send the manuscript. "Dass ich ohne vorgängigen Abschluss des Geschäftes das Manuscript nicht ausliefere, werden Dieselben in der Betrachtung billigen, dass ich den Schillerischen Erben, worunter sich zwei Frauenzimmer befinden, responsable bin und ich mich daher auf alle Fälle vorzusehen habe." No matter how laudable Goethe's intentions may have been in wishing to help the family of his friend, he could scarcely have expressed himself more tactlessly, and this letter gave rise to anger and confusion on the part of Cotta and a misunderstanding on both sides which almost brought about the end of their association.

Cotta, deeply hurt, waited until February 11, 1828, before replying in a long letter which we quote here in its entirety:

E. E. geehrtes Schreiben vom 17. Dezember darf ich nicht länger unbeantwortet lassen. Der Eindruck, den dasselbe auf mein durch sehr bittere Erfahrungen ohnedies sehr schwer gestimmtes Gemüth machte, will ich nicht zu beschreiben suchen, genug, dass es der Schlusstein eines sehr kummervollen Jahres war.

Ich betrachte zunächst die Thatsache, so wie sie durch gedachtes Schreiben sich mir darstellt: ein Manuscript von den ersten Schriftstellern ist mir für Reichsthaler 8,000 angeboten— die Einsicht desselben wird mir nicht zugestanden, denn nur wenn ich die verlangte Summe übermache, soll diess Manuscript abgehen.

Ich gebe gerne zu, dass ein Werk von solchen Meistern, durch

Ihre Redaction sanctioniert, eine Ausnahme von der gewöhnlichen Regel—eine Waare vorher zu beschauen ehe man sie kauft und bezahlt—rechtfertige, und, dass die in dem Schreiben angegebenen Daten zur Berechnung der Ausdehnung des Werkes genügen konnten und würden, wenn Vertrauen gegen Vertrauen gesezt wäre.—Wie aber, wenn von der einen Seite Vertrauen vorausgesezt wird, von der andern Seite ein Misstrauen gezeigt wird, das zu den ungewöhnlichen gehört? Sollte, vorausgesezt es wäre ein ganz fremder, unbekannter Verleger, diesem es verdacht werden können, wenn er, ehe er die Reichsthaler 8,000 zahlte, den Wunsch ausspräche, das Manuscript einzusehen, um nach seinen buchhändlerischen Erfahrungen seinen Calcul darnach zu machen, da ein Honorar von solcher Bedeutung, (der Factor der Druckerei schäzt das Ganze nach den gegebenen Daten auf 4 mässige etwas weitläuf gedruckte Bände)—doch gewiss einiges Bedenken rechtfertigt.

Wenn aber ein solches Misstrauen nicht einem fremden unbekannten Verleger gezeigt wird, sondern einem Mann der mehr als dreyssig Jahre in Verbindung steht und der nie, nur einen Tag seine Geldobliegenheiten unerfüllt liess, wie unerwartet muss diesem ein solches Misstrauen erscheinen?

Aber mir bey meinem reinen Bewusstseyn, bey meinem rechtlichen Gefühl musste es mehr als unerwartet, es musste mir die schmerzhafteste Erfahrung seyn.

Denn ich darf und muss mir das Zeugniss geben, dass ich auch nicht den entferntesten Anlass auch nur zum leisesten Verdacht oder Misstrauen Ihnen gegeben, ja, dass ich mein Benehmen der ganzen Welt vorlegen darf, und dass mir das Zeugniss nicht entstehen kann, mit Rechtlichkeit, Edelmuth und Aufopferung die Verhältnisse des Verlegers gegen Verfasser beachtet und behandelt zu haben.

Denn während der mehr als dreyssigjährigen Verbindung wurde mit der grössten Gewissenhaftigkeit jede Verbindlichkeit erfüllt, jedem Wunsch entgegengekommen; galt es wirkliche vorausgesehene Opfer, ich brachte sie gerne, denn ich schäzte das Verhältniss höher als blosse Finanzspeculanten es betrachten würden. Beweiss nur der Verlag von Morphologie, und Kunst und Alterthum, von welchen ich einen Verlust von fl. 9000 nachweisen kann—und welches Opfer brachte ich damals, als ich im Jahre 1811 noch 2 Jahre das Verlagsrecht hatte und dasselbe zur

Herausgabe einer Taschenausgabe benuzen wollte?—Auf Ihren Wunsch verzichtete ich auf diese Speculation.—Weigerte ich mich im Jahre 1812, zu den vertragsmäsigen Reichsthaler 1500 für den Band des Biographischen Werkes noch Reichsthaler 500 nachzutragen?

Doch wir wollen diess Alles nicht betrachten, wir wollen nur die Vorgänge bey dem letzten Vertrag zur Beurtheilung meiner Denk- und Handlungsweise uns ins Gedächtniss rufen:

als mir geschrieben wurde, es hätten sich mehrere Gebote für die Herausgabe der sämmtlichen Werke angemeldet und, dass ich das Meinige zu machen hätte.—Welche Antwort hätte ich darauf geben konnen? Krafft des Contracts folgende: es möge mir das höchste Gebot mitgetheilt werden, und ich würde mich dann darauf erklären, ob ich in dasselbige einstehen wolle, da mir bey gleichem Gebot nach dem Vertrag das Vorzugsrecht gebühre. —Welche Antwort gab ich aber: ich könnte dieses Recht ansprechen, ich erbiete mich aber, Reichsthaler 10,000 mehr als das höchste Gebot zu geben—ich konnte, ich durfte erwarten, mit umgehender Post diess höchste Gebot zu erfahren und, dass mir mit Reichsthaler 10,000 Aufschlag das Verlagsrecht wieder zustehe.—Jeder Tag der verzögerten Antwort war für mich bedenklich—Monate aber vergiengen, ohne dass ich Antwort erhielt, und ich entzog mich dennoch auch weiteren Wünschen nicht.—

Die erhaltenen Briefe sprechen für mich, und in meiner Brust trage ich ein stolzes Gefühl über den Grund meiner damaligen Handlungsweise—Sollte diess und Alles in sittlicher und ökonomischer Hinsicht nicht hinreichend gewesen seyn ein solches Misstrauen niederzuschlagen?—

Zwar wird bemerkt: die Verbindlichkeit gegen die Schiller'schen Erben, worunter sich zwey Frauenzimmer befänden, erfodere, sich vorzusehen—Was die auf diesen Theil fallenden Reichsthaler 400 betrifft, so hat der Vormund Reichsthaler 2250— der Sohn Ernst Reichsthaler 700, Carl Reichsthaler 1132.8, die beyden Töchter Reichsthaler 500 und (fl. 800) 444.10 erhalten, die ganze Familie bereits 5026.18—mithin Reichsthaler 1026.18 mehr als ihren Antheil.

Ob der Mann, der bey bisherigen mehr als fl. 160,000 betragenden Zahlungen nie im geringsten Rückstand blieb, der stets einen offenen Credit bey Frege verfügte und erhielt, so ängstlich zu behandeln war!—will ich nur berühren und bemerken, dass ich mir das Zurückrufen aller dieser Thatsachen, das Durchlesen und Berühren der darauf Bezug habenden Briefe erlauben musste, weil der Mensch, wenn er sich durch ein Ereigniss tief ergriffen und unglüklich fühlt, sich—je schuldloser und unbefleckter er sein Leben wünscht—an seinen inneren Richter wendet, sich fragend und prüfend: womit hast Du diess verdient? und findet er im Ganzen und Besonderen nichts, was auf ihn schuldet, die Tropfen dieses stillen aber wichtigsten Trostes gerne in den Kelch fallen lässt, dessen bitteren Trank er nicht an sich vorbeygehen lassen konnte, weil er unbewusst und unabwendbar eingegeben wurde.

Ich habe diesen Trost, aber die bittere Erfahrung wird mir in's Grab geleiten. Was die früheren Besprechungen betrifft, so habe ich auf die gegebene Nachricht, "dass sich nichts in den Papieren der Frau v. Schiller vorfinde" die meinigen nachgesucht. Die copirten Anlagen von der vorgeschlagenen und von mir genehmigten Uebereinkunft vom 25. März 1824 so wie die Copie der Schreiben von F. v. Schiller beweiset, dass wir längst übereingekommen und, dass erst nach dieser Uebereinkunft die verewigte Freundin die Briefe abgab.

Ich muss diese mir theure Erklärung als ein Vermächtniss heiliger Art ansehen und wie wir schon vor 3½ Jahren diese Sache als ausgemacht betrachteten, so muss ich sie noch betrachten und erbitte mir daher die Termine der Zahlung und Ablieferung.

Mögen Sie nun nach dieser offenen vor meinem Inneren gleichsam abgelegten Erklärung auch Ihr Inneres sprechen lassen —denn bey allem meinem Kummer kann ich mich doch und will ich auch nicht mich eines Gedankens entschlagen, dem nämlich, dass Ihr Inneres in jenem Schreiben sich nicht aussprach.

Mit den herzlichsten Wünschen für Ihr Wohl und den unwandelbarsten Gesinnungen. . . .[56]

Not until March 8 did Goethe reply, and then not to Cotta, but in an angry letter to Boisserée. Referring to Cotta's statement that the Schiller family had already received payment of more than their share of the honorarium, Goethe said: "Man hat auf eine unverantwortliche Weise gehandelt, dass man mir die an die v. Schiller'schen geleisteten Vorschüsse und Stückzahlungen verheimlichte und mich dadurch in dem Irrthum liess, als sey ich gegen jene noch wegen des ganzen

Betrags ihres Antheils am Honorar verpflichtet und responsabel, weshalb ich denn auch mit allem Recht das Manuscript zurückhielt, bis ich nicht sowohl mich als vielmehr sie befriedigt wüsste." In his reply of March 17, Boisserée tried to soothe Goethe by telling him of the great difficulties Cotta had been having in his recent business ventures, so that he was hardly himself.[57] When Ernst von Schiller discovered what was holding up publication, he wrote to Goethe's son, denying emphatically that Cotta had paid him or any member of his family for the correspondence. He claimed that what Cotta must have meant to say was that the money he had paid was an installment on the honorarium for Schiller's collected works, for which Cotta and the Schillers had a contract.[58] In June he wrote again to August von Goethe, saying that he had investigated carefully, and that this was indeed the case, Cotta, in his indignation, having apparently not made himself at all clear to Goethe.[59] It seems, then, that it was a case of misunderstanding. Goethe's stubbornness and lack of tact aroused Cotta, whose unclear statement had only made matters worse.

Whether Cotta's appeal to Goethe's sense of fair play had any effect is difficult to say, but on the same day that Goethe wrote so indignantly to Boisserée he enclosed a signed contract for publication of the letters, and a month later the manuscript was in Cotta's hands. The first volume appeared in November 1828, and Goethe was honest enough to tell Cotta on the 30th that he was pleased with the way it had turned out.[60]

Thus ended another chapter in the Goethe-Cotta relationship. It must have been an unpleasant experience for all concerned. Goethe's understandable desire to protect the interests of the Schiller family is laudable. However, his firm belief that Cotta, as a representative of the publishing profession, was depriving him of his rights, prevented him from seeing Cotta's side of the picture.[61]

From 1829 onwards Goethe's publishing confined itself largely to scientific material. Publication of the *Ausgabe letzter Hand* proceeded at a fairly regular pace, but not as quickly as Goethe would have liked. Most of the correspondence during this time was with Reichel rather than Cotta and deals largely with details of the printing and delivery of the various volumes of the edition. The danger of piracy was not entirely overcome but gave no great cause for worry. Cotta feared that an edition might appear in Holland, and asked Goethe to request a Dutch copyright,[62] but the latter wrote back pessimistically on February 13, 1830, not seeing his way clear to take the necessary steps. However, he had, shortly before, written to Max von Gagern, youngest son of the Netherlands delegate to the Vienna Congress, to ask him whether it would be possible to obtain a copyright for Luxemburg. Von Gagern's answer offered some hope for this copyright, but as Goethe told Cotta on March 12, 1830, one for the Netherlands seemed out of the question.

In the early autumn of the same year Goethe had to cope with one last piracy scare. He heard from Reichel that the Hamburg publishing house of Schuberth and Niemeyer was advertising a cheap edition of his works.[63] Hastily he wrote to Heinrich Küstner, a Leipzig banker who was the diplomatic representative of Weimar in Saxony, sending him a copy of the advertisement, and Küstner made the necessary representations in Leipzig. However, before the decree banning the publication and sale could be made public, the Leipzig branch of the Hamburg firm announced that the edition was none other than the *Ausgabe letzter Hand.* Küstner claimed that someone, sensing a good practical joke, had advertised it as something new.

The correspondence with Cotta had already dwindled, and with the end of 1830 any discussion of Goethe's relationship with his publishers may be brought to an end. Not unnaturally, Goethe wished to rest, particularly since the task of providing for his family had been accomplished. He wanted no more arguments, whether with publishers or anyone else. Writing to von Müller on May 21, 1830, he expressed himself thus: "In meinen hohen Jahren muss die unverbrüchliche Maxime seyn: durchaus und unter jeder Bedingung im Frieden zu leben; ich möchte, um keinen Preis, bey irgend einer Contestation, sie habe einen politischen, literarischen, moralischen Anlass, als thätig mitwirkend erscheinen."

The little time that was left to Goethe following the decision to republish the *Metamorphose der Pflanzen* was marked by occasional letters to Cotta, written for the most part to commemorate anniversaries of one kind or another. None of the bitterness and friction is apparent; on the contrary, we find only expressions of the highest esteem, and, one could almost say, of affection. But this is not surprising. Let us remember that Goethe tried his best to keep his relationship with Cotta on two entirely separate levels. In spite of his advanced age and his repeated emphasis on his desire for rest, there can be little doubt that had he found it necessary to become involved with Cotta again on a business footing he would have treated him no differently than before, if the negotiations had been on a large scale. He had given in to Cotta on the subject of the payment for the *Metamorphose der Pflanzen* with no argument, no haggling. But that, after all, could not be considered a major venture.

The unpleasant incidents which marred the long association of Goethe and Cotta might have been avoided had they thrashed out their differences in personal conference more often. But as we have seen, for Goethe this was asking too much. Not only did he find it difficult to make friends easily, but his distrust of people with whom he thought he was going to have to bargain made it impossible for him to sit down with Cotta and settle their problems. He felt himself so aristocratic, so far above the level of persons whose living depended upon financial dealings, large or small, that he avoided contact with businessmen wherever possible.

To sum up, we can begin by noting that Goethe's association with Cotta had, at the start, all the earmarks of a most successful one. That it ended successfully in a material way is apparent, but the personal feelings existing between the two men were not always friendly. The few years following the publication of the Schiller-Goethe correspondence may be discounted, since the business association was to all intents and purposes over, and the carefully worded, formal letters of esteem which make up the correspondence in those years do not tell the whole story.

Looking at the whole extent of their association, we may say that there was no real friction between the two until that day in Carlsbad when Goethe discovered the Armbruster edition of his works. This discovery, purely by accident, as it seemed, forced Cotta to suggest a new and definitive edition. If we then look more carefully at the relationship, we can see that there were minor matters which caused temporary breaks. The first of these is important—the insistence on Goethe's part that Cotta publish *Cellini* if he wished the poems for his *Taschenbuch auf das Jahr 1804*—since it shows that no matter what happened between 1804 and 1832, there was virtually no change in Goethe's attitude towards Cotta. When he first made Cotta's acquaintance, he was impressed, as we have seen from letters to both Schiller and Cotta himself. But this favorable impression was not such that it forced him to feel that Cotta deserved more generous treatment than any other publisher.

It is worth noting again that the periods between the publication of the collected works were marked by relative tranquillity. The only serious clash in these periods when individual works were making their appearance was Goethe's ultimatum regarding *Dichtung und Wahrheit,* and Cotta's surrender to his demands made the matter much less serious than it would have been. Perhaps the explanation for Goethe's seeming casualness about these separately published works lies in the fact that he knew that they would later be preserved in their proper places in an edition of his collected works. On the other hand, his anxiety, particularly in the later years, to rush some of them into print would stem quite naturally from his fear that he might not live to supervise another edition.

It is difficult to say just why Goethe delayed so long in telling Cotta that he was planning to publish the *Ausgabe letzter Hand*. Perhaps he kept it a secret, while informing friends of his intentions, hoping that Cotta would make the suggestion, whereby he would be in a position to accept or reject Cotta's proposals. At any rate, he did not feel that he was not being quite frank and honest towards his publisher, as we can see from his accusations that Cotta had been dealing behind his back when he discovered the Viennese edition of his works in Carlsbad. We may ask ourselves at this point whether Cotta's actions in allowing Armbruster to stretch his edition to twenty-six volumes were justified, and in a purely objective light, the answer would probably have to be in the negative. However, if, as has been suggested, Armbruster was blackmailing Cotta with the threat of suspending the *Allgemeine Zeitung,* we may claim that these were extenuating circumstances. The only shadow on Cotta's otherwise flawless behavior is his not informing Goethe of what had happened between him and Armbruster. To this puzzle there is no satisfactory solution, other than the thought that Cotta may have chosen to risk Goethe's anger in order to keep his beloved journal alive. However, one cannot help thinking that had Cotta told Goethe earlier of his predicament, Goethe might have been less inclined to accuse Cotta of not keeping faith with him.

When attempting to evaluate Goethe's conduct in relation to these final negotiations with Cotta one should bear in mind the point that he had long since become set in his ways. It would perhaps be not unnatural for anyone to resent Cotta's failure to keep him informed on developments in Austria, but for Goethe in particular this was but proof of what he had suspected all along. It is difficult to imagine that he would have later behaved differently even if the whole incident had never taken place.

Presumably, since Cotta had placed himself in an awkward position, Goethe then felt justified in using any means at his disposal to show that he was not the man to take things lying down. His insistence that in divulging the amounts of the various offers which had been made by other publishers he would be guilty of a breach of faith was a weapon which he found convenient to use. Nevertheless, one has the feeling that he underestimated Cotta—or else was not far-sighted enough to realize that Cotta could exercise legal prerogatives. At any rate, he was determined to carry his fight to the end, to force Cotta into an agreement, hence his fencing and side-stepping. Three things eventually combined to make him relent: the realization that Cotta could take the matter to court if he so desired, Boisserée's persuasive insistence that it would be unwise to change horses in the middle of the stream, and the fact that he himself was no longer up to the physical and mental strain of prolonged bickering. The acquisition of his copyright too had assured him that no publisher could poach upon his preserves—not even Cotta.

One might be easily tempted to paint Goethe completely black in discussing his association with Cotta were it not for two points: the matter of Cotta's hesitancy in divulging to him the full scope of his dealings with Armbruster and the fact that Goethe's actions were governed by something which was an integral part of him. We would be unjust in condemning him absolutely for actions which were more or less natural to him. And yet it is unfortunate that during the many years of his relationship with Cotta he made no real attempt to see whether there might have been another course of action or another angle from which he could have judged his publisher. He got along quite well with Cotta socially, albeit they were never intimate friends; it is regrettable that their business association was kept on an entirely different level.

Chapter 5

In the tenth book of *Dichtung und Wahrheit,* where Goethe describes the attitude of Herder relative to the unsuccessful operation on his eye, he digresses to a brief discussion of various kinds of ingratitude. He makes a distinction between what he terms "Nichtdankbarkeit, Undank und Widerwillen gegen den Dank." It is possible to see traces of all these characteristics in Goethe himself, and they may account in some measure for his singular conduct towards his publishers by forming part of the sovereign attitude which was so strong in him. "Nichtdankbarkeit," he claims, is part of everyone's make-up. By the time an individual has shown gratitude to "der Sonne und der Erde, Gott und der Natur, Vorvordern und Eltern, Freunden und Gesellen," he is incapable of thanking other well-wishers. This is due to what Goethe terms "eine glückliche leichtsinnige Vergessenheit des Widerwärtigen wie des Erfreulichen." If, however, this is carried too far, one begins to regard benefactors as strangers, whom it is permissible to hurt if by hurting them one's own ends are advanced. This Goethe calls ingratitude. An aversion to expressing gratitude, he says, is rare, and is found only in men who are unusually gifted. What such men give is of a high intellectual nature, what they receive for it is material, and hence they assume that the compensation cannot measure up to the gift.

In this same discussion he goes on to say: "Ich bin von Natur so wenig dankbar als irgend ein Mensch, und beim Vergessen empfangenes Guten konnte das heftige Gefühl eines augenblicklichen Verhältnisses mich sehr leicht zum Undank verleiten." That this happened, and happened often, has been sufficiently illustrated by what has been said here. In fact, this momentary resentment occurred so frequently that it became almost permanent and developed into a life-long mistrust on the one hand and an attitude of sovereignty on the other. It was helped by two things: the impression which Behrisch made upon him in Leipzig, and the fact that Goethe felt himself on a higher level, both socially and intellectually, than men of business in general. Just as Johann Caspar Goethe entertained a dislike of hostels and their owners, but had to make use of them, so his son cultivated a similar dislike for the publishing profession—and was likewise forced to deal with it all his life.

That Behrisch should have influenced his thinking so strongly is hardly surprising when we consider how impressionable a youth Goethe was. But even in youth it is possible that a contempt for businessmen, men who made a living by bargaining and contracting, was already inherent in his thinking. Goethe, who was to make so much of aristocracy in *Wilhelm Meister,* and who was impressed by the aristocracy, was himself aristocratic enough to look down upon merchants.

These statements may not seem to be supported by what has been said about the publication of Goethe's early works. In fact, as we have seen, he had very little experience with the publishing world before going to Weimar. His reactions in those early years were a mixture of carefree extravagance and caution about the publication of his work. The warnings of Behrisch and his own inhibitions regarding publishers were as yet only partly developed, but it would be a mistake to assume that these warnings were planted in barren soil. Since Goethe was not directly concerned with making money from his writing, indeed was not even sure whether he could continue to write, there is hardly any reason why we should expect him to be consistent. Piracy meant little or nothing to him, and he blew hot and cold by turns on the subject of seeing his work in print.

We are able to glean even less information on his feelings during the ten years following his arrival in Weimar, but again there are adequate reasons for this. If he were any less inconsistent in his reactions during this period, it was because he published so little. But if, as we assume, the seeds of his dislike for the publishing profession had not yet begun to take root within him, the broader conception of his superiority to the merchant type probably developed. In the early Weimar years, when he acted in the capacity of general factotum to the court, he must have come into contact with dozens of persons with whom he had to deal in a business way. He must have had to bargain and bicker and argue—often about monetary matters, and hence it is not surprising that his dislike for such tasks increased. This would account for the frequent use of mediators between him and his publishers and also for his apparent desire to keep his business and his social activities in two separate channels.

His association with Göschen revived the suspicions which Behrisch had planted in his mind, and from the beginning he was on his guard. We can say without reservation that from this time onward the conviction grew in Goethe that publishers were individuals whose objective in life was to gain as much as possible for themselves at the expense of an author. And although the reasons for this conviction lay in part within Goethe himself, we must take into consideration the unsavory reputation of the book trade in Germany at the time. One thing which did impress him was the ridiculously low stipends with which writers were regarded for their efforts. Goethe was the last person who tended to hide his light under a bushel, and since he was so very much convinced of his worth he was determined from the start not to be satisfied with anything less than what he considered a fair remuneration. Having made a name for himself in the literary world at a relatively early age, he felt that if one publisher rejected his demands, there was always another who would be only too glad to accept. It was as though he thought the time had come to teach the publishing profession a lesson, and that he was the man who could do it. Naturally, if this were the case, every move which a publisher made was suspect, and out of this developed the obsession that all publishers were doing their best to deceive him and deprive him of what was rightfully his.

To these two feelings of distrust and superiority is due in large measure the domineering and inconsiderate attitude which Goethe adopted towards Göschen. There can be no doubt that he realized full well that Göschen needed him badly, and from the beginning of their association he capitalized on this fact. Goethe was convinced of his own ability as a man of business, but he was not quite experienced enough, nor did he know himself well enough. For in signing with Göschen the first contract by which he had ever entered into an agreement with a publisher, he underestimated his ability to live up to the contract. And, when the burden of the agreement began to weigh heavily upon him, he became irritated, not at himself, but at Göschen. As a result, he found himself forced to argue and to justify his annoyance. This was what he wished least of all to do with a man to whom he felt so immeasurably superior.

He was relieved to find himself dealing with Unger, and their relationship was a relatively cordial one. With no contract to bind him, and with a publisher who bowed down before him, he was in his element. Not that he felt any more well disposed towards publishers as a result of this association, but here was a man who knew his place, who made Goethe feel that this was the relationship which ought to exist between author and publisher. And in the case of Vieweg, Goethe had reached the point where he felt quite justified in demanding a large sum for a manuscript, sight unseen. The fact that Vieweg accepted his demands served only as a further justification of his notion that one should treat a prospective publisher as one would treat a servant. But again his vaunted business sense failed him when Vieweg asked permission to publish yet another edition of *Hermann und Dorothea*. His vague, noncommittal reply was practically an invitation to Vieweg to proceed. And when the inevitable occurred, it was simply further confirmation of Goethe's already deep-seated mistrust. He hardly stopped to think that a definite negative answer might have made all the difference in the world.

Up to this point, then, we have seen that although Goethe's opinion of the book trade was in some measure justified, the difficulties which had confronted him stemmed largely from himself, and were due in part to a youthful impressionability, in part to an a priori theory which he was never willing to give up, or even modify. As for Cotta, however, he was momentarily nonplussed. He was forced to admit that Cotta did not conform to his conception of a publisher. But Goethe could never forget that Cotta was a businessman—and therefore not wholly to be trusted. Hence the careful scrutiny of their contracts and the use of mediators whenever possible.

It is worth while noting once more that during the periods of Goethe's publication of individual works, the association with Cotta was comparatively amicable. This relationship appears to be a throwback to that with Unger, where there was no definite time limit, no deadline to meet, and no real contract. This was the type of business association which suited Goethe best, since it left him free to complete his works at leisure and to devote his time to something else if need be. A binding contract seems to have been something into which he entered with mixed feelings. He was anxious to reach an agreement because it would usually assure him of forcing his terms on the publisher, but at the same time he looked upon a contract with some distaste, because it tied him down, and, what was even more unpleasant, involved argumentation and disputes.

One can hardly call Goethe's treatment of Cotta—or of any other of his publishers—exemplary. The attitude which he so often adopted was under no circumstances conducive to real friendship and mutual trust. We may perhaps make excuses for him by taking into consideration two things: the fact that he was an intellectual giant and that he was born into a time when the lack of legal machinery and the unscrupulousness of many persons connected with publishing made it difficult to have confidence in the profession. But, on the other hand, since he was one of the most human of all human beings, he could have tried to adjust himself to the feelings and the personalities of others—particularly Cotta. Regardless of his genius, his high opinion of his own worth, and his conviction that others owed him respect, he might have made a greater effort to credit a man like Cotta with some virtues. Leaving the literary genius of Goethe and the business genius of Cotta out of the question, he would not have needed to step down from his lofty perch of aristocracy in order to meet Cotta on equal ground. But the mistrust of the publishing profession was something which never left him. Granted that the conduct of many publishers was far from exemplary, rarely did Goethe make an effort to see the good in those with whom he was closely associated.

We should not underestimate the importance of the personalities involved in these various associations. In the case of Göschen's relations with Goethe we may speak of a clash of personalities, meaning not so much that the two men were very different but rather that their aims and objectives were similar. Unger's personality is pale and almost lifeless compared with Goethe's, but it was precisely this passive attitude which pleased Goethe and which no doubt helped Unger's cause. Cotta, who in his own way was as ambitious and aggressive as Göschen and as tactful as Unger, was more intelligent than either of them. He was a man whom Goethe could not browbeat into submission, but he could afford to give in when he saw that prolonged argument would only injure their association. He could and did stand up for what he thought were his rights as well as Goethe could, and in the last analysis theirs was a case of an irresistible force meeting an immovable object, with both sides eventually making concessions to reach an agreement.

Appendix

(Note: Section A supplements material in Chapter 1; Sections B, C, and D supplement Chapter 3; Sections E-K refer to Chapter 4.)

A. Goethe's Contract with Göschen

Der Herr Geheimrath von Goethe giebt Buchhandler Herrn Georg Joachim Göschen in Leipzig seine Schriften in Verlag und zwar folgendermassen.

1.

Die nunmehr gedruckte und hierbey geheftete Ankündigung enthält das Verzeichnis derjenigen bisher sowohl gedruckten als ungedruckten Schriften, von welchen auch das bedingte Versprechen, dass der Verfasser, wenn es ihm an Musse nicht fehlen sollte, das möglichste thun wird um den vier letzten Bänden eine vollkommenere Gestalt zu geben, als es der Anzeige nach geschehen würde. Es versteht sich von selbst, dass alsdann, wenn einige der noch unvollendeten Stücke vollendet würden, andere dagegen aus der Sammlung bleiben müssten, wovon man gegenwärtig nichts sagen kann; genug, dass es des Verfassers Absicht ist, die vier letzten Bände denen vier ersten an innerm Gehalt soviel als möglich gleich zu machen.

2.

Die zwey ersten Bände liegen zur Ablieferung bereit; zwey können um Michaelis abgeliefert werden, die vier letzten verspricht man nicht vor Ostern, doch wird man es sich durchaus zur Pflicht rechnen, den Herrn Verleger nicht aufzuhalten.

3.

Ueberhaupt möchten drei Bände gedruckter, fünf ungedruckter Schriften gerechnet werden können.

4.

Dafür erhälte der Herr Verfasser überhaupt: Zweitausend Rthlr. in Louis d'or zu 5 Rthlrn. welches Honorarium gegen das Manuscript, wie solches abgeliefert wird, theilweise zu bezahlen ist.

5.

An jeder künftigen Auflage behält der Autor sein Recht und zwar:

1. dass keine ohne sein Wissen und Einwilligung gemacht werden kann.

2. dass ihm jeder Bogen Druck mit Einem Louis d'or neuere zukommende Aufsätze mit 3 Louis d'ors bezahlt werden.

3. Vergreift sich aber eine neue Ausgabe innerhalb drei Jahren und ist sie 2000 stark, so zahlt der Verleger oder seine Erben an den Verfasser oder seine Erben 2½ Rthlr. von den schon gedruckt gewesenen Werken nach.

4. Wäre die erste oder irgend eine folgende Ausgabe vergriffen, und es wäre die Convenienz des Hrn. Göschen oder seine Erben nicht, eine neue zu veranstalten, so bleibt es dem Herrn Verfasser oder den Seinigen unbenommen einen andern Verleger zu suchen.

6.

Das Format ist wie das vorige Himburgische, klein Octav mit deutschen Lettern, neue Schrift auf schönes Schreibpapier sauber und geschmackvoll gedruckt. Die Anzahl der Exemplarien verlangt der Verfasser nach geendigten Druck zu wissen, ob er gleich den Verleger nicht einschränken will.

7.

Ingleichen gibt der Herr Verfasser zu, dass eine Auflage in gross Oktav für Liebhaber schöner Exemplare gedruckt werde, zu welcher er ein nochmals genau revidirtes Exemplar der kleinen Ausgabe dem Herrn Verleger zustellen wird, damit auch der geringste Fehler, der sich allenfalls in die kleinere Auflage einschleichen könnte, aus der grossen entfernt bleibe. Wie starck die grosse Auflage gemacht worden, wird dem Verfasser nach deren Beendigung angezeigt.

8.

Von jeder dieser beyden Auflagen bedingt sich der Verfasser Vierzig Exemplare aus, zwanzig auf Holländisch Papier und zwanzig auf ordinäres Schreibpapier, zusammen achtzig Exemplare, in englischem Band, jeden Band besonders gebunden.

9.

Uebrigens überlässt der Verfasser die Einrichtung des Drucks und die Verschönerung des Werkes ganz dem Verleger; doch wünscht er einige Proben von Prosa und Versen gedruckt zu sehen; dazu der Verleger einige Stellen nach Belieben wählen kann.

10.

Seine folgenden Schriften wird der Hr. Verfasser Hrn. Göschen vor Andern anbiethen, behält sich aber nach den Umständen vor deshalb besondere Bedingungen zu machen.

11.

Nach vollendetem Druck werden die Manuscripte in welchem Zustand sie auch seyn mögen, dem Herrn Verfasser zurückgegeben.

So geschehen, Carlsbad, d. 2. Sept. 1786.

J. W. von Goethe

B. "Promemoria" to Cotta, May 1, 1805

Unterzeichneter hat die Absicht, seine Schriften neu herauszugeben, und zwar sollte von keiner vollendeten Prachtausgabe, vielmehr von einer saubern und geschmackvollen Handausgabe mit deutschen Lettern die Rede seyn. Enthalten wurde dieselbe alles was von meinen ästhetischen Arbeiten einige Dauer verdient. Manches ungedruckte ist hinzugefügt.

Zu vertheilen wären in zwölf Bände folgende Werke, ungefähr folgender Massen:

I

Vermischte Gedichte.

II

Wilhelm Meister.

III

Wilhelm Meister.

IV

Die Laune des Verliebten
Die Mitschuldigen
Die Geschwister
Mahomet
Tancred
Elpenor. Fragment.

V

Götz von Berlichingen
Egmont
Stella
Clavigo

VI

Iphigenie
Tasso
Eugenie

VII

Claudine
Erwin und Elmire
Jery und Bätely
Lila
Scherz, List und Rache
Zauberflöte. Zweyter Theil. Fragment.

VIII

Kophta
Triumph der Empfindsamkeit
Vögel
Bürgergeneral
Was wir bringen

IX

Reinecke Fuchs
Hermann und Dorothea
Achilleis.

X

Faust. Fragment.
Puppenspiel

XI

Werther

XII

Desgleichen.

Wie die Lieferungen einzutheilen und was sonst noch weiter zu verabreden wäre, ist fernerer Ueberlegung anheim gegeben. Das neue ist roth unterstrichen.

G. [oethe]

C. Rough Draft of the Goethe-Cotta Contract for the
1816 Edition of the Works

ENTWURF EINES CONTRACTS

Der Herr Geheime Rath von Goethe zu Weimar überlässt Herrn Doctor Cotta in Stuttgart die abermalige Ausgabe seiner Werke, und zwar wird Folgendes bestimmt und bedingt:

1) Die Zahl der Bände ist auf zwanzig festgesetzt, den Inhalt derselben weist beyliegendes Verzeichniss.

2) Die Zahl der Lieferungen hängt von dem Herrn Verleger ab, so wie die Termine derselben.

3) Das Verlags-Recht wird bis Ostern 1823 zugestanden; nach Ablauf dieses Termins behält der Herr Verleger das Vorrecht vor andern unter gleichen Bedingungen.

4) Der Verfasser bedingt sich dagegen die Summe von Sechzehn Tausend Thalern, sächsisch.

5) Die Zahlungs-Termine können auf die Lieferungs-Termine gesetzt werden. Man ist nicht abgeneigt einen Theil der Summe gegen 5 pro Cent Interesse und halbjährige jedem Theil freystehende Aufständigung stehen zu lassen, wenn daraus für den Herrn Verleger einige Bequemlichkeit entspränge.

6) Die Zahl der Exemplarien bleibt wie bey den bisherigen Verlags-Artikeln auf 44 festgesetzt, wovon 20 velin-Papier, 24 auf Schreib-Papier.

s.m.

Weimar, d. 20. Febr. 1815   Goethe.

D. Final Draft of the Goethe-Cotta Contract for the 1816 Edition of the Works

CONTRACT

Der Herr Geh. Rath von Goethe zu Weimar überlässt Herrn Dr. Cotta in Stuttgart die abermalige Ausgabe seiner Werke, und zwar wird folgendes bestimmt und bedingt:

1) Die Zahl der Bände wird auf zwanzig festgesetzt, den Inhalt derselben verweiset beyliegendes Verzeichnis.

2) Sie erscheinen in fünf Lieferungen, je von acht Monaten.

3) Das Verlagsrecht wird bis Ostern 1823 zugestanden, nach Ablauf dieses Termins behält der Herr Verleger das Vorrecht vor andern unter gleichen Bedingungen.

4) Der Verfasser bedingt sich dagegen die Summe von Sechzehn Tausend Thalern sächsisch.

5) Die Zahlungs Termine sind bey jeder Lieferung Drey Tausend Thaler—bey der letzten Lieferung

Vier Tausend Thaler

Was der Herr Verfasser von diesen Zahlungen nicht bezieht bleibt gegen 5 pr. Cent jährl. Interessen, und halbjahrige, jedem Theil freystehende Aufkündigung stehen.

6) Die Zahl der Exemplarien bleibt wie bey den bisherigen Verlagsartikeln auf 44 festgesetzt, wovon 20 Velinpapier, 24 auf Schreibpapier.

144

Wiesbaden d. 15. Juni 1815.   J. W. v. Goethe.

ad 5) Der Erste Zahlungstermin trifft mit dem ersten also Ostern 1815 zusammen, sodann werden die Zahlungstermine von acht zu acht Monaten gerechnet.

eod.   G.

E. Rough Draft of the Goethe-Cotta Contract
for the *Ausgabe letzter Hand*

ENTWURF I

1. Die neue Ausgabe von Goethischer Werke,

2. bestehend aus vierzig Bänden nach dem schon mitgetheilten Inhaltsverzeichniss,

3. wird der von Cottaischen Buchhandlung in Stuttgart, überlassen und zwar:

4. auf Zwölf Jahre.

5. Der Betrag des Honorars ist vorerst auf Sechzig Tausend Thaler sächsisch, nicht unter 1/6 festgesetzt.

6. Man bedingt sich jedoch ausser vorgedachter Summe fünf Tausend Thaler bei Unterschrift des Contracts.

7. Das Uebrige in Terminen, nach Maassgabe der Ablieferung des Manuscripts.

8. Sind Zwanzig Tausend Exemplare abgesetzt so tritt eine neue Berechnung ein;

9. von denen hiernächst abgesetzten Zehn Tausend Exemplaren kommen dem Autor abermals
Zwanzig Tausend Thaler in vorerwähnten Münzsorten zu Gute;

10. und so fort bei jeden abermaligen Absatz von Zehn Tausend Exemplaren.

11. Ob nun gleich hierdurch der Zeitcontract aufgehoben scheint, so ist dieses jedoch nicht die Meinung sondern zu Anfang des neunten Jahres treten beide theilnehmende Partheien zusammen und contrahiren aufs Neue nach Verabredung in welchem Maasse der Contract fortgesetzt werden soll.

12. Wie die von Goethische Familie von der Zahl der Subscribenten und sonst abgesetzten Exemplaren unterrichtet werden könne wäre auszumitteln, welches wohl am leichtesten durch besondere Buchführung über dieses Geschäft geschehen kann.

13. Der Subscriptionspreiss der 40 Bände wäre mässig zu setzen, 14-16 Thaler wie schon erwähnt worden. Weimar d. 20. Septbr. 1825.

145

F. Rough Draft of the Goethe-Cotta Contract, January 8, 1826

ENTWURF

1. Die neue Ausgabe von Goethischer Werke,
2. bestehend aus vierzig Bänden nach dem schon mitgetheilten Inhalts-Verzeichniss,
3. wird der J. G. Cotta'schen Buchhandlung zu Stuttgart überlassen und zwar
4. auf zwölf Jahre d. h. von Ostern 1826 bis Ostern 1838.
5. Der Betrag des Honorars ist vorerst auf
   sechzigtausend Thaler sächsisch
   nicht unter 1/6 Stücken festgesetzt.
6. Man bedingt sich jedoch ausser vorgedachter Summe noch fünftausend Thaler in vorerwähnten Münzsorten bey Unterschrift des Contracts.
7. Die ganze Ausgabe wird in *vier* Jahren zu vollenden seyn, jährlich zwey Lieferungen jede zu fünf Bänden, welche der Autor successiv abreicht, dagegen würde
8. von Messe zu Messe der achte Theil des Honorars mit 7500 Thalern sächsisch, und zwar Ostern 1826 zum erstenmal, gezahlt.
9. Sind zwanzigtausend Exemplare abgesetzt, so tritt eine neue Berechnung ein und es werden
10. von jeden hiernächst abgesetzten eintausend Exemplaren dem Autor immer dreytausend Thaler, in vorerwähnten Münzsorten gezahlt, und so fort.
11. Von den einzeln zu druckenden Theilen überlässt man dem Herrn Verleger jeden Vortheil allein und behält sich nur eine noch zu bestimmende Anzahl Freyexemplare vor.
12. Diese neue Ausgabe von 40 Bänden besteht
    A. in einer anständigen Octav-Ausgabe,
    B. in einer Taschen-Ausgabe, bey beiden behält
sich der Autor die Einwirkung bey Wahl des Formats, Papiers und der Lettern vor.
13. Ob nun gleich durch den Punct 10 der Zeitcontract aufgehoben scheint, so ist dieses jedoch nicht der Fall, sondern zu Anfang des 9. Jahres, treten beide theilnehmende Parteien zusammen und contrahiren aufs neue, nach Verabredung, in welcher Maasse der Contract festgesetzt werden soll. Käme alsdann, wie nicht wahrscheinlich, eine Vereinigung nicht zu Stande, so muss bey eröffneter Concurrenz dem Autor frey bleiben dem Mehr- oder Minderbietenden seine Rechte anzuvertrauen.

14. Die Uebersicht über dieses ganze Geschäft wird durch eine doppelte Buchführung in noch näher zu bestimmender Maasse bedingt.

15. Der Subscriptionspreis wäre auf *circa* 20 Gulden festzusetzen.

16. Bedingt man sich die herkömmlichen Freyexemplare, wie solches auch bey der früheren Ausgabe statt gefunden.

Schliesslich behält man sich vor, die beide contrahirende Theile gegen einander sicher stellenden juristischen Formen, in dem nach erfolgter Zustimmung in vorstehende Puncte förmlich zu entwerfenden Contract, noch nachzubringen.

pp.

G. The Prussian Copyright of 1826

Wir Friedrich Wilhelm III
von Gottes Gnaden
König von Preussen etc.

Von unsern Ministerien des Innern und der auswärtigen Angelegenheiten ist Uns das Ansuchen des Grossherzoglich Sachsen-Weimarisch Staats-Ministers

Johann Wolfgang von Goethe

um Ertheilung eines ausdrücklichen Privilegiums zum Schutz wider den Nachdruck der von ihm beabsichtigten neuen und bereicherten Ausgabe seiner Schriften, so wie gegen den Handel mit einem etwa auswärts unternommenen Nachdrucks derselben, vorgetragen worden. Wenn Wir nun die ausgezeichneten Verdienste des Nachsuchenden um die deutsche Litteratur in Erwägung genommen und ihm gern einen Beweis Unserer Anerkennung derselben zu erkennen geben wollen, so haben Wir diesem Gesuche nachgegeben und ertheilen hierauf demselben, so wie seinen Erben und Cessionarien, nicht weniger dem rechtmässigen Verleger dieser neuen und bereicherten Ausgabe das gebetene ausdrückliche Privilegium stempel- und kostenfrei, dergestalt, dass Wir den Druck und den Handel mit etwa auswärts veranstalteten Nachdrücken sowohl vorerwähnter vollständigen neuen Ausgabe der von Goetheschen Werke, als wie auch einzelner Theile oder Auszüge daraus, in sämmtlichen Provinzen Unseres Staats, mithin nicht nur in denjenigen, wo die Vorschriften des Allgemeinen Landrechts für die Preussischen Staaten zur Anwendung zu bringen sind, sondern auch in denjenigen Landestheilen, wo das französische Recht oder andere Gesetzgebungen

147

noch in Gültigkeit bestehen, hiemit ausdrücklich verbieten, und wollen, dass jede Entgegenhandlung dieses Privilegiums, welches dieser Ausgabe der Goetheschen Werke vorzudrucken oder nach seinem Inhalte auf oder hinter dem Titel-Blatte zu vermerken ist, zu den gesetzlich bestimmten Entschädigungs-Ansprüchen berechtigen und mit denjenigen Strafen belegt werden soll, welche der Nachdruck inländischer Verlags-Artikel und der Händel mit auswärts gedruckten Büchern nach sich zieht.

Nach dieser Unserer Allerhöchsten Willensmeinung hat sich ein jeder Unserer Unterthanen, den es angeht, insonderheit aber sämmtliche Gerichte und Polizey-Behörden genau zu achten.

So gegeben *Berlin,* den 23. Januar 1826

Friedrich Wilhelm

Schuckmann.   Bernstorff.

H. Goethe's Letter of Thanks to Friedrich Wilhelm III

Allerdurchlauchtigster

Grossmächtigster Allergnädigster

König und Herr.

Die von Ew. Königlichen Majestät mir zugewendete Landes-herrliche Gnade ist von einer solchen Bedeutung, dass ich sie mit dem vollkommen freudigen Danke, wie geschieht, zu empfangen kaum fähig seyn würde, wäre mir nicht schon längst das Glück beschieden, mich denen bey-zählen zu dürfen, die Allerhöchstihro Glorreichem Wirken in treuer Gesinnung angehören. Denn das Wichtigste, was von Kunst und Wissenschaft in Ew. Königl. Majestät weitumfassenden Reiche sich bewegt und schafft, liess mich seit langen Jahren nicht ohne Kenntniss und Antheil.

Männer, welche unter Allerhöchstem Schutz nach einsichtigen Befehl arbeitend das Treffliche vollbringen, solche standen von früh an mit mir in traulichen Verhältnissen, und durch fort-dauernde Wechselwirkung ist eine geistige Mitbürgerschaft ein-geleitet, welche über Zeit und Art hinaus ein gegenseitiges Glück befördert.

In diesem Sinne darf ich daher mit einiger Beruhigung des Vorzugs geniessen, dass Allerhöchstdieselben mich als einen getreuen Angeeigneten betrachten und mir gleiche, ja ausgezeich-nete Rechte mit den Ihrigen verleihen wollen.

Indem ich nun aufs Neue in solchem Umfange Ew. Königl. Majestät verpflichtet werde, so kann mir kein anderer Wunsch übrig bleiben, als der: Es möge die so hoch begünstigte Ausgabe meiner sämmtlichten literarischen Arbeiten in den lebendigen Thatkreis, der Allerhöchstdieselben umgiebt, aufgenommen, dort in ihrer Art einen wünschenswerthen Einfluss verbreiten, um so auch auf die übrige Welt einzuwirken, die von keinem Guten, das unter Ew. Majestät belebendem Scepter sich hervorthut und waltet, jemals ausgeschlossen worden.

Ehrfurchtsvoll
Ew. Königl. Majestät

Weimar *allerunterthänigster Diener*

den 15. März 1826. *Johann Wolfgang von Goethe.*

I. Friedrich Wilhelm's Reply to Goethe
An den würklichen Geheimen Rath von Goethe in Weimar.

Mein Herr Geheimer Rath von Goethe!

Bey dem grossen Gewinn, den Kunst und Wissenschaft durch Ihre Werke erhalten haben, konnte Ihnen die Anerkennung gerechten Anspruchs auf die diesen Werken in ganz Deutschland zu Theil gewordene landesherrliche Vergünstigung nicht entstehen; um so angenehmer ist es Mir indessen gewesen, aus Ihrer Eingabe vom 15ten v. [on] M. [ärz] zu ersehen, dass die Erfüllung Ihrer Erwartungen Sie zu der Mir gewidmeten Dankbesiegung aufgefordert hat. Ich verbleibe des Herrn Geheimen Raths

Wohlgeneigter

Potsdam den 2. April 1826. (gez.) *Friedrich Wilhelm.*

J. Goethe's Contract with Cotta for the Publication of the Schiller-Goethe Correspondence
Uebereinkunft wegen Herausgabe der Goethe-Schillerischen Correspondenz.

1. Das Honorar für das redigirte Manuscript wird auf

Acht Tausend Thaler

festgesetzt.

2. Die J. G. Cotta'sche Buchhandlung erklärt: Dass nach Anweis ihrer Bücher und Rechnungen die v. Schillerischen Erben für die denenselben gebührende Hälfte von Vier Tausend Thalern durch Vorschüsse und Stückzahlungen vollkommen befriedigt sind.

3. Gedachte Buchhandlung verpflichtet sich, hierüber ein legales Zeugniss von Seiten der Schillerischen Erben beyzubringen, wodurch zugleich Unterzeichneter aller ferneren Ansprüche entbunden, auch gebilligt würde, dass der Verlagsbuchhandlung das gesammte Manuscript inzwischen eingehändigt worden.

4. Die J. G. Cotta'sche Buchhandlung zahlt die auf die Goethesche Seite fallende Hälfte an

Vier Tausend Thalern

in zwey Terminen, den erstern Ostern, den zweyten Michael 1828.

5. Das Verlagsrecht wird auf zwölf Jahre zugestanden und zwar von der Erscheinung an des Werks im Publicum.

6. Die erste Ausgabe wird in Octav veranstaltet: sollte man jedoch in der Folge eine Taschenausgabe belieben, so wird man alsdann über den zu entrichtenden Nachschuss des Honorars Uebereinkunft zu treffen haben.

7. Frey-Exemplare erhalten

die Goetheschen:

Velinpapier 12

Gewöhnlich Papier 8

Mit den Schillerischen wird die Verlagshandlung unmittelbar deshalb übereinkommen.

8. Sobald Unterzeichneter eine mit dem Vorstehenden übereinstimmende schriftliche Zusicherung erhält, geht alsobald das vollständige Manuscript an die Verlagsbuchhandlung ab.

9. Die Aushängebogen werden successiv, wie sie die Presse verlassen, anher gesendet.

Weimar den 8. März. 1828   J. W. v. Goethe.

K. Summary of the Goethe-Cotta Contract
for the *Ausgabe letzter Hand*

Note: This contract is summarized in English because of the author's inability to get permission to reproduce the original (now at the Schiller Nationalmuseum in Marbach) in full.

The contract between Goethe and Cotta contained the following general provisions:

1. Cotta was to have the rights for twelve years.

2. Cotta was to publish a de luxe octavo edition as well as the regular edition.

3. Goethe was to receive 60,000 (Saxon) taler, and additional royalties for all copies sold above 20,000.

4. Cotta agreed to complete publication of the 40 volumes of the edition within four years.

The contract was signed by both Goethe and his son August on March 3, 1826.

Notes

Chapter 1

1. *Goethes Werke,* herausgegeben im Auftrage der Grossherzogin Sophie von Sachsen (Weimar, 1887-1914), I, 27, 131 f. Hereafter cited as *W. A.* In order to simplify printing, and because of the inconsistencies of eighteenth and early nineteenth century orthography, I have everywhere reproduced *sz* as *ss*.

2. I doubt very much that his request that no copy be made had anything to do with a fear of pirating; he was simply shy because he thought that his work was not mature enough.

3. In his *Zur Morphologie,* Goethe, speaking of his experiences in having it published, wrote: "Abermals befand ich mich also in derselben Lage, wie jene da ich dem Buchhändler *Fleischer* meine *Mitschuldigen* anbot; diessmal aber liess ich mich nicht sogleich abschrecken" (*W. A.,* II, 6, 134).

4. Here too, in his contact with the artists, and in his own artistic efforts, Goethe undoubtedly acquired much of the information which made him so particular about illustrations of his works in later years.

5. For an accurate and exhaustive study of this subject, see J. A. Goldfriedrich, *Geschichte des deutschen Buchhandels* (Leipzig, 1886-1913).

6. "He simply finds, when he looks into himself, that he is changeable, lacking in steadiness of mood or thought, and he uses the suggestive chameleon image to describe his condition" (Barker Fairley, *A Study of Goethe* [Oxford, 1947], p. 5).

7. H. Bräuning-Oktavio, *Der Erstdruck von Goethes Götz von Berlichingen* (Darmstadt, 1923), p. 15.

8. Boie wrote to Götter: "Hier wird er so gelesen, dass von 50 Exemplaren, die hierher kamen kein einziges mehr da ist" (Bräuning-Oktavio, *Götz,* p. 17).

9. Cf. letter to Sophie von La Roche, December 23, 1774.

10. *W. A.,* I, 28, 202: "Weil wir aber, bei unsern beschränkten Verhältnissen, die Exemplare nicht schnell genug nach allen Orten zu vertheilen vermochten, so erschien plötzlich ein Nachdruck; und da überdiess gegen unsere Aussendungen freilich sobald keine Erstattung, am allerwenigsten eine baare, zurückerfolgen konnte: so war ich, als Haussohn, dessen Casse nicht in reichlichen Umständen sein konnte, zu einer Zeit wo man mir von allen Seiten her viel Aufmerksamkeit, ja sogar vielen Beifall erwies, höchst verlegen, wie ich nur das Papier bezahlen sollte, auf welchem ich die Welt mit meinem Talent bekannt gemacht hatte."

11. Goethe refers to this as a *Nachdruck.* Cf. also Morris, *Der junge Goethe* (Leipzig, 1910) VI, 253, hereafter cited as "Morris."

12. On the title-page the place of publication of *Zwo wichtige . . . Biblische Fragen* is given as "Lindau am Bodensee," but this is fictitious. There is divided opinion among scholars as to the place of publication of both works, some saying that they were published by Deinet in Frankfurt, others that they were a product of the Merck-Goethe collaboration in Darmstadt.

13. Max Rieger, *Klinger in der Sturm- und Drangperiode* (Darmstadt, 1880), p. 25.

14. Rieger, *Klinger,* p. 26.

15. Karl Wagner, *Briefe aus dem Freundeskreise von Goethe, Herder, Höpfner und Merck* (Leipzig, 1847), pp. 101-102.

16. Erich Schmidt, *Lenz und Klinger: Zwei Dichter der Geniezeit* (Berlin, 1878), p. 54.

17. *W. A.*, I, 28, 327.

18. *W. A.*, I, 28, 227. Goethe's memory failed him here. Cornelia was married on November 1, 1773, and her brother did not send the MS of *Werther* to Weygand until May of 1774. In fact, he did not begin writing it until February of that year.

19. *GJB*, XXV, 217.

20. Morris, VI, 352.

21. Karl Wagner, *Briefe an und von Johann Heinrich Merck* (Darmstadt, 1838), p. 53.

22. (Amsterdam, 1773).

23. L.-S. Mercier, *Neuer Versuch über die Schauspielkunst: Aus dem Französischen: Mit einem Anhang aus Goethes Brieftasche* (Leipzig, 1776), pp. 484 f.

24. *Gesänge, mit Begleitung des Klaviers* (Leipzig und Winterthür, 1777). This was probably edited by Kayser.

25. Viscount Goschen, *Georg Joachim Goschen: Publisher and Printer* (New York, 1903), I, 166. Christian Gottfried Körner was also a partner in the firm. Fritz Hünich states that Bertuch's part was entirely unknown to Goethe, and that indeed it did not come to light until some hundred years later. (*Goethe-Kalender auf das Jahr 1925*, p. 103.)

26. *W. A.*, IV, 7, 234. Göschen used this letter of Goethe's for advertising purposes in various periodicals and distributed a number of broadsides accompanied by a short introduction.

27. Goschen, I, 165. There appears to be some confusion in regard to this letter. In 1881 it was first printed in *GJB*, II, 395, as follows: "Leipzig, 17. Juni, 1786. In der That ist 3 Louisd'or (für den Bogen) alles Mögliche, was Goethe erwarten kann. In der That ist es schon etwas hart für uns und wenn Goethe mit zwei Carlsd'or zufrieden ist, so haben wir es immer noch nicht wohlfeil. Doch nehmen müssen wir es auch zu 3 Louisd'or und müssen nachher desto lauter und anhaltender trommeln." Viscount Goschen translated thus: "Three louis d'or is certainly the utmost that Goethe can possibly expect. Indeed, even this is rather hard for U. [Unger], and if Goethe is satisfied with two carl d'or, U. will still not have it cheap. Nevertheless U. must take it even at three louis d'or, and must afterwards beat the drum all the more loudly and continuously." He then continued: "But although Göschen said that U. [Unger] could not refuse, the bargain was not struck."

Deneke [*Goethes Schriften bei Göschen 1787-1790*, in *Göttinger Beiträge zur Goethebibliographie Vierter* (Göttingen, 1909), p. 1], who gives Goschen as one of his principal sources, says: "Die gesellschaftliche Verbindung zwischen Goethe und Göschen war von Bertuch vermittelt worden, nachdem Goethe vorher mit dem Berliner Verleger Johann Friedrich Unger ergebnislos über die Übernahme des Verlages verhandelt hatte."

In order to try to resolve this problem I wrote to the late Prof. Wahl, then Director of the Goethe-Schiller Archiv in Weimar. He was kind enough to send me a photostat of the letter in question. Although it is true that the letters which the GJB interprets as *uns* are not very clear, the later use of *wir* is unmistakable. It is probable, then, that *uns* is what Göschen had written, or that he may have had some special character which he used when meaning *uns*. It is thus by no means certain that Unger was approached before Göschen.

28. *GJB*, II, 396.

29. *GJB*, II, 398.

30. Göschen tried desperately to see Goethe in Carlsbad, but his anxiety to get to Prague and Vienna in order to solicit subscriptions and to acquire

privileges forced him to leave the day Goethe arrived. As far as we know, the two never met. (Cf. *GJB*, II, 399.)

31. Cf. *W. A.*, IV, 8, 25, for a letter to Herder telling him of his instructions to Göschen.

32. Letter to Bertuch, *GJB*, II, 399. Göschen, to whom the threat of piracy was like a red rag to a bull, could not resist addressing himself to pirate publishers at the end of his advertisement for Goethe's works. He wrote the following "open letter":

"An die Herren Nachdrucker.

"Ich kann es mir zwar leicht vorstellen, dass die hier angekündigten Werke auch eine ganz artige Spekulation für Sie seyn werden; allein erlauben Sie mir doch, meine Herren, Ihnen ehe Sie zum Werk schreiten, die Versicherung zu geben, dass ich auch schon ganz artige Massregeln gegen Sie genommen habe, und Muth genug besitze mit Aufopferung meines ganzen Vortheils Ihre Hofnungen zu Wasser zu machen, wenn Sie mich in meinem rechtmässigen Erwerbe durch Ihre unrechtmässige Industrie zu stöhren gedenken. Besitzen Sie noch einigen guten Namen in der Welt, so heben Sie ihn gewiss durch eine solche Unternehmung gänzlich auf. Sie sollen so blamirt werden, dass ihr eigenes Weib, Ihr eigenes Kind Sie mit Verachtung ansehen und kein ehrlicher Mann mit Ihnen aus einem Kruge trinken soll" (Deneke, p. 6).

33. *GJB*, II, 400.

34. *GJB*, II, 400.

35. *GJB*, II, 400.

36. Göschen had good reason to be anxious. By Easter 1787 there were only 550 names on the subscription list instead of the 1,000 which he and Bertuch had expected.

37. *GJB*, II, 403.

38. *GJB*, II, 404.

39. Goethe sent it to Seidel with instructions to show it to Bertuch.

40. *GJB*, II, 405.

41. Otto Deneke, *Die Einzeldrucke Goethe'scher Werke bei Göschen 1787-1790*, in *Göttinger Beiträge zur Goethebibliographie Fünfter* (Göttingen, 1909), p. 19.

42. Goschen, I, 267.

43. *GJB*, II, 408.

44. Deneke, *Göttinger Beiträge Vierter*, p. 25. We have already noticed how energetically Göschen reacted to the mere thought of piracy, and he printed polemics against it four times during his publication of Goethe's works. One of these appears on the page preceding the dedication in the first volume, and Goethe, with justification, thought it a trifle out of place.

45. *W. A.*, II, 6, 133.

46. *Die Metamorphose der Pflanzen* was first published by Ettinger in Gotha, 1791.

47. *W. A.*, II, 6, 133.

48. *GJB*, VI, 102.

49. *GJB*, VI, 105.

50. *W. A.*, II, 6, 133.

51. Without Goethe's permission, Göschen also published two editions of *Clavigo* and *Götz von Berlichingen*, three of *Werther* and *Egmont*, five of *Tasso*, and seven of *Iphigenie.* Waltraud Hagen, *Die Gesamt- und Einzeldrucke von Goethes Werken* (Berlin, 1956), pp. 72 ff.

52. Flodoard Freiherr von Biedermann, *Goethes Gespräche* (Leipzig, 1909), II, 426. Hereafter cited as "Biedermann, Gespräche."

53. In Vol. 1 of the 1806 Cotta edition there is a group of poems under the heading "Gelegenheitsgedichte," but these are not personal.

54. It is quite true, as Trunz and others point out, that the rather loose composition of the novel permitted the insertion of this material in the third volume, but in their haste to justify Goethe's actions, they all gloss over the fact that he admitted that he was "padding."

Chapter 2

1. Flodoard Freiherr von Biedermann, *Johann Friedrich Unger in Verkehr mit Goethe und Schiller* (Berlin, 1927), p. xix. (Hereafter cited as "Biedermann.") All dated letters from Unger are to be found in this volume.

2. Biedermann, p. xxxvi.

3. Biedermann, p. 178, notes: "Ueber die von Unger gedruckte *Iphigenie* liess sich nichts ermitteln, weder in Weimar, noch in anderen deutschen öffentlichen Bibliotheken konnten Stücke nachgewiesen werden."

Here, at the very beginning of their association, we run into a peculiar problem. Was Unger guilty of piracy? We know that Göschen had the rights to *Iphigenie*. On May 12 Göschen told Goethe that he had heard of Unger's commission from the Duke and that he would like to do the work himself. Goethe apparently put him off by offering to let him print a special edition of *Tasso,* which Göschen gratefully accepted, not missing an opportunity to criticize the accuracy of Unger's work. The *Tasso* edition in question appeared in 1790. In the letter to Bertuch, Unger speaks of "gütiger Rat" coming too late. This may have been advice from Bertuch to stop the printing for fear of accusations of piracy, but Göschen apparently did not press the matter.

4. No record exists of what he said to Unger on the subject.

5. Biedermann, p. 47.

6. Biedermann, p. 48.

7. Biedermann, p. 10. The play was probably *Die Aufgeregten,* which remained a fragment.

8. *Iphigenia in Tauris: A Tragedy,* written originally in German by J. W. von Goethe. Printed at the Norfolk Press by J. Crouse and W. Stevenson. For J. Johnson, St. Paul's Church-Yard, London. MDCCXCIII. (Trans. by William Taylor of Norwich.)

9. On August 23, 1794, Schiller wrote to Goethe suggesting that it would be most advantageous for the proposed *Horen* if Goethe would publish his *Wilhelm Meister* in it in serial form. Goethe answered somewhat regretfully on August 27 that Unger had already begun publication. It was, however, definitely to Goethe's advantage to have the novel in book form, since it would not only have a larger and quicker circulation than if published serially but also be more profitable.

10. Goethe, in 1795, was planning a trip to Italy, where he was to join Meyer. (Letter to Schiller, Sept. 14, 1795.) He mentioned it again to Jacobi on June 12, 1796, and to Friederike Unger on June 13. On Aug. 10, 1797, he wrote Knebel that he no longer had any desire to make the journey.

11. Biedermann, p. 64. DePernay, an "emigré" in Weimar, had sent the translation to Goethe, but had not mentioned publication. Unger rejected it on the grounds that he had no business connections in France.

12. Biedermann, p. 181.

13. Friedrich von Schiller, *Briefe,* hrsg. Fritz Jonas (Stuttgart, 1892-96), VI, 32.

14. Steinhilber (p. 76) surmises that Goethe may have been aware that Unger had, without permission, issued more than one edition of individual works.

15. When Schiller was asked by Unger to support the journal *Irene,* he became extremely annoyed, and wrote to Goethe on March 17, 1802, saying

that he would like to send Unger a sharp reply. Goethe's answer of March 19 seems to be directed at the publishing profession in general rather than Unger in particular as Steinhilber (p. 77) claims: "Ich wünsche Ihnen einen recht guten Humor und eine recht derbe Faust, wenn Sie auf die Irenische Einladung antworten. Es wäre recht schön, wenn Ihnen eine Epistel glückte, die auf alle das Packzeug passte, dem ich immer grössern Hass widme und gelobe."

16. Unger's widow wrote to Goethe on Jan. 26, 1805, to say that she would be happy to take over any work that Goethe might have intended her husband to publish. Goethe thought highly of a farce which Friederike Unger had written, entitled *Mondkaiser,* and had it performed several times in Weimar.

17. L. Geiger, *Zeitschrift für Bücherfreunde,* hrsg. Fedor von Zobeltitz, 1897, Jahrgang 1, pp. 143-149.

18. L. Gerhardt, *Karl August Böttiger und Georg Joachim Göschen im Briefwechsel* (Leipzig, 1911), p. 13.

19. Gerhardt, p. 13.

20. *W. A.,* IV, 12, 396.

21. Biedermann, *Gespräche,* I, 256. The idealistic Schiller, feeling that it was an honor for Vieweg, wrote Goethe on Jan. 31, 1797: "Das Werk wird einen glänzenden Absatz haben, und bei solchen Schriften sollte der Verleger billigst keinen Profit zu machen suchen, sondern sich mit der Ehre begnügen. Mit schlechten Büchern mag er reich werden."

22. Albert Schäffle, *Cotta* (Berlin, 1895), p. 29.

23. Schäffle, *Cotta,* p. 41.

24. Wilhelm Vollmer, *Briefwechsel zwischen Schiller und Cotta* (Stuttgart, 1878), p. 284. (Except where otherwise noted, all dated correspondence between Schiller and Cotta refers to this volume.)

25. *W. A.,* IV, 14, 267. Cotta had printed 1,300 copies of the first issue, of which about 450 had been sold; he needed a sale of at least 1,000 in order to meet the costs of publication.

26. Vollmer, p. 342.

27. According to Vollmer, receipts show that Goethe had received sixty Carolin for this, the fifth issue. For the first and second he had received the same amount, so that it would appear that Cotta had not accepted Goethe's offer.

28. In March 1800 Friedrich Wilmans of Bremen presented Goethe with a case of assorted wines and a request for a contribution to his *Taschenbuch auf das Jahr 1801.* Goethe replied on May 30 that he felt he could not refuse, and sent him *Der Zauberflöte,* Zweyter Theil, which appeared in 1802. His one other publication had been *Die guten Frauen,* which appeared in the *Taschenbuch für Damen auf das Jahr 1801,* and which he had written at Cotta's request.

Chapter 3

1. Vollmer, p. 534.

2. Goethe's final demand was 10,000 taler.

3. Vollmer, p. 534 (note), claims that the demand of 10,000 taler "stimmt so ziemlich überein" with the original price.

4. Date of Cotta's letter unknown.

5. Christian August Vulpius, Goethe's brother-in-law.

6. Johann Daniel Falk, writer and director of an academy in Weimar.

7. *W. A.,* IV, 19, 269.

8. In a letter of October 7, Goethe wrote: ". . . so muss ich nochmals

ausdrücklich bitten, das, was unsre politische Existenz betrifft und nicht von mir kommt, von Ihren Blättern abzuweisen."

9. This was not the only instance when Goethe inveighed against one of Cotta's journals. The *Morgenblatt für gebildete Stände*, edited by Johann Haug, carried on in 1808 a battle against the sonnet. Goethe was particularly interested in the form at the time, and took umbrage at the attacks. In the issue of March 11 there appeared an article entitled: *Schreiben eines Studierenden auf der Universität ------ an seinen Vater, den Baudirektor R------ zu B------*. This rather cheap attack on romantic philosophy ended with the caricature of a sonnet, entitled *Das Posthorn*. One of the lines reads:

"Am jüngsten Tage, wenn das Posthorn kräht,"

and quite coincidentally, it would seem, one of Goethe's more successful sonnets written about this time begins:

"Am jüngsten Tag, wenn die Posaunen schallen."

Whether Goethe assumed that this was a direct attack upon himself cannot be determined with any certainty, but a month later, on April 9, he wrote indignantly to Cotta, informing the publisher that he had sent several sonnets by friends to other journals for publication. Nor was it simply the articles against the sonnet which annoyed him. He thought that the *Morgenblatt* was devoting its pages to trivialities, and that it was beneath his dignity to contribute to it, although he had previously done so. He had, apparently, no real animosity toward Haug, who was a relatively harmless person, but was angered that Cotta had seemingly turned against him.

10. Vollmer, p. 563.

11. *W. A.*, IV, 21, 462.

12. Vollmer, p. 691.

13. *W. A.*, IV, 21, 210.

14. Cotta had apparently visited Goethe in the spring of 1811, and must have encouraged him in his work, because on May 14 Goethe wrote him as follows: "Die Lust, meine biographische Arbeit fortzusetzen, hat sich seit Ihrer Gegenwart noch bei mir vermehrt." Maria Fehling, *Briefe an Cotta* (Stuttgart u. Berlin, 1925), I, 110.

15. *W. A.*, IV, 22, 452. In 1808-11 there appeared in Vienna a 15-volume pirated edition of *Goethes sämmtliche Schriften*.

16. *W. A.*, IV, 22, 455.

17. *W. A.*, IV, 22, 494.

18. *W. A.*, IV, 23, 440.

19. From 5: *Theatralische Gelegenheitsgedichte;* from 8: *Maskenzüge, Carlsbader Gedichte,* and *Epimenides Erwachen;* from 9: *Das Neueste aus Plundersweilern, Satyros,* and *Epilog zu Schillers Glocke;* from 10: *Die Zeichen der Zeit;* from 11: *Pandora;* from 13: *Die guten Weiber.*

20. *W. A.*, IV, 28, 245.

21. On October 12, 1810, a ruling had been passed in Vienna that no work which had been censored in MS in that city could be pirated there. *Allgemeine Zeitung,* 1894, Beilage 14, p. 6.

Chapter 4

1. Goethe called him "der Mainzer Humorist" and thought quite highly of his sonnets. He was an army major, aide to General von Krauseneck and a prolific poet. In 1814 he visited Goethe for the first time in Weimar and saw him frequently thereafter in Wiesbaden and Carlsbad.

2. Christoph Friedrich Ludwig Schultz, state councillor and government representative at the University of Berlin, who had taken a great interest in Goethe's *Farbenlehre*. He met Goethe in 1814, visited him often, and tried to persuade him to let Humblot in Berlin publish the *Ausgabe letzter Hand*.

3. Leopold von Henning, lecturer in philosophy at the University of Berlin.

4. H. H. Houben, *J. P. Eckermann: Sein Leben für Goethe* (Leipzig, 1925), I, 126.

5. *Goethes Werke.* Original-Ausgabe. Wien. In Carl Armbrusters Buchhandlung. 1816-1821. Stuttgart: In der J. G. Cotta'schen Buchhandlung. Otto Rauscher writes that J. S. Grüner, proprietor of the bookstore in Carlsbad, claimed that Goethe was not unimpressed by this edition, saying that it was a good one. He cites, in *Chronik des Wiener Goethe-Vereins*, xxxix, 23 ff., the volume: *Goethes Briefwechsel mit Joseph Sebastian Grüner und Joseph Stanislaus Zauper,* hrsg. August Sauer (Prag, 1917), p. 344.

6. Laistner, *Armbruster und die Wiener Goethe-Ausgabe,* Beilage zur *Allgemeinen Zeitung,* Beilage-Nummer 14 (Stuttgart und München, 1894), pp. 4-7. What follows is taken largely from this report.

7. *W. A.,* IV, 38, 292.

8. *W. A.,* IV, 27, 225.

9. In May, 1825, Goethe wrote to Boisserée: "Seit dem unseligen Wiener Nachdruck hat sich von beyden Seiten kein rechtes Vertrauen wieder einfinden wollen."

10. *W. A.,* IV, 38, 311.

11. *W. A.,* I, 29, 87.

12. So far as is known, Macklot did not pirate any of Goethe's works.

13. That to exchange his poems for money was repulsive to him.

14. *W. A.,* I, 29, 16.

15. *W. A.,* I, 36, 61.

16. *W. A.,* IV, 22, 494.

17. *W. A.,* IV, 26, 421.

18. On the basis of a remark by Goethe in a letter to Nagler of September 18, 1825, Gaedertz assumes that Goethe had met him in Weimar. Cf. *Bei Goethe zu Gaste* (Leipzig, 1900), p. 317. Hereafter cited as "Gaedertz."

19. Gaedertz, pp. 323 ff.

20. He reported also that Hannover, Mecklenburg-Schwerin, Baden, and Hessen had already sent favorable answers. In a letter to von Beust of December 18 he said that Braunschweig, Brussels, and Luxemburg had not yet come to a decision.

21. This document, as well as Goethe's letter of thanks to the King of Prussia and Friedrich Wilhelm's reply, is reproduced in the Appendix.

22. *W. A.,* IV, 39, 347.

23. On May 4 and 14, 1825, the brothers Heinrich and Friedrich Brockhaus visited Goethe in Weimar. On the basis of discussions there they received the impression that Goethe, who was very pleasant, was strongly inclined to allow them to publish the edition. With August von Goethe they even settled tentatively on a fee of 50,000 taler and rights for ten years. After a month had passed with no word from Weimar, they heard that Goethe now wanted to negotiate on the basis of the number of copies sold, which would raise the price. Dubiously, they agreed and asked for a quick settlement. August again asked for time to consider other offers, and suddenly, in answer to queries, the Brockhaus firm heard on September 8 that Goethe had signed a contract with Cotta. Actually, there was on that date no binding contract and they knew this. They then hastily offered 70,000 taler, but without success.

24. Goethe asked Zelter on July 6 what he thought of Reimer and on July 11 received the following reply: "Er hat vieles unternommen was ihm gelungen zu sein scheint, doch ein Geschäft mit ihm würde ich in sicherer Form fassen, nachdem was ich so hier und dort vernommen." On August

14, Goethe's son sent Reimer a noncommittal answer, saying: "Uebrigens gebietet die von Ihnen selbst anerkannte Wichtigkeit Umsicht und Ueberlegung; es handelt sich davon, das ökonomische Wohl unserer Familie auf lange Jahre zu sichern."

25. *W. A.*, IV, 40, 347.

26. Vollmer, p. xi.

27. Cotta to Schiller, November 13, 1797: "Erhalten Sie seine gütige Stimmung für mich!" Schiller to Cotta, November 22: "Von Ihnen spricht er mit ungemeiner Achtung und Zuneigung. Dass ich Ihnen bei ihm nicht schaden werde, werden Sie mir aufs Wort glauben."

28. As it turned out, neither Goethe nor Cotta committed himself on the payment until printing was well under way.

29. He expressed very much the same idea to Rochlitz in 1824, when Weygand in Leipzig asked if he might issue a new edition of *Werther*. Goethe wrote on April 30: "Sie sehen leicht dass es in diesem Falle unerfreulich wäre direct zu handeln und vielleicht gar zu markten, darum ich Dieselben ersuche die Vermittlung über sich zu nehmen."

30. On the same day Boisserée wrote to his brother: "Das Verhältnis von Cotta mit Goethe scheint sehr bedenklich; ich höre von allen Seiten, der alte Herr habe mit Cotta gebrochen. . . . Ich werde durch diese Gerüchte darin bestärkt, dass Cotta sich auf eine ungeschickte Weise muss ausgedruckt haben. . . ." Wilhelm Bode, *Goethe in vertraulichen Briefen seiner Zeitgenossen* (Berlin, 1923), III, 238.

31. Apparently the unprofitable venture with *Götz* had left no lasting impression on Goethe, since he was obviously considering the possibility of becoming his own publisher. On June 9 the bookdealer Wilhelm Hoffmann in Weimar had told August that his father could count on 280,000 taler, based on an edition of 30,000 copies, if he decided to publish it himself. *W. A.*, IV, 40, 349.

32. *W. A.*, IV, 40, 349.

33. He did not know that the news of the granting of the copyright, in the form of a letter from Metternich, was already on its way to Weimar. Cf. letter to Gentz, September 16, 1825.

34. Cf. letter to Goethe, August 23: "Der Verkauf gegen ein gewisses Honorar auf bestimmte Zeit oder für eine bestimmte Ausgabe bleibt immer das Angemessenste. . . ." *Sulpiz Boisserée* (Stuttgart, 1862), II, 392. Hereafter cited as "Boisserée."

35. Cf. August's letter of September 18 to Joseph Max, in which the latter was informed that Goethe had definitely decided to deal with Cotta (*W. A.*, IV, 40, 391).

36. On August 29 and again on September 24 Schlesinger in Berlin had offered 60,000 taler (*W. A.*, IV, 40, 387). On October 25 the "Bureau des Correspondenzblattes für Kaufleute" in Gotha had offered 200,000 taler, to be paid by a company set up specifically for the purpose of publishing the edition (*W. A.*, IV, 40, 391).

37. Boisserée, II, 400.

38. Cf. letter of January 3, 1826 (Boisserée, II, 401).

39. On November 19, 1825, the brothers Brockhaus made their bid of 70,000 taler. Heyer in Giessen on November 13 and the Hahn firm in Hannover on November 19 each offered 150,000 gulden. This is roughly the equivalent of 95,000 taler (*W. A.*, IV, 40, 442).

40. Boisserée, II, 410 f.

41. Cotta eventually made a very respectable profit on the *Ausgabe letzter Hand*, but on the basis of past experience with Goethe's works he was not in a position to predict this with any certainty.

42. Boisserée, II, 411.

43. On February 3 Goethe found time to express his gratitude to Boisserée in the following words: "Doch eigentlich ist es der schon längst gekannte, geprüfte Freund Sulpiz, der uns das unmöglichste Bauwerck als vollendet vor Sinn und Seele bringt, der uns durch das Labyrinth uralte Gewölbe und Kreuzgänge zu klarem Anblick durchführt. . . . Und dieser wendet nun sein tätiges Wohlwollen gegen mich und das Meinige!

"Sie haben sich, lassen Sie es mich gerade zu sagen, so klug als tüchtig, so edel als grandios gezeigt, und ich fange nur an mich zu prüfen ob ich meinen Dank bis an Ihre Leistung steigern kann."

44. *W. A.*, IV, 41, 354.

45. *W. A.*, IV, 41, 363. Goethe felt that the inclusion of *Helena* was over and above what he had promised Cotta, and hence asked for special compensation in the form of eighteen copies of the latest *Faust* edition which he could present to friends (*W. A.*, IV, 41, 252).

46. *W. A.*, IV, 42, 396.

47. To Göttling on January 17, 1829, he spoke of *Wilhelm Meisters Wanderjahre* as "dieser sisyphische Stein." Writing to Riemer on February 9, he referred to it as "der lästige Alp."

48. Vollmer, p. 571.

49. Goethe asked von Humboldt on June 22, 1823, to bring with him on a proposed visit to Weimar any correspondence he may have had with Schiller.

50. This was unfortunately not available to me.

51. According to Cotta's books, Goethe received 4,000 taler, and the Schiller family a like sum (Vollmer, pp. 690 and 693).

52. Vollmer, p. 571. Cf. also her letter to Goethe of March 24, in *Literarischer Nachlass der Frau Caroline von Wolzogen,* hrsg. B. Abeken (Leipzig, 1848), I, 439.

53. In May 1826 Caroline von Wolzogen said to Ernst von Schiller that in a conversation Goethe had told her of his being astute in his contract with Cotta. It had been decided that there would be four volumes, for which Cotta would pay 2,000 taler each. If Cotta also wished to put out a smaller edition, it would cost him another 2,000 taler. Goethe was pleased, she went on, that the agreement of 1825 was still valid, and he said that he found it necessary to open up a sharp offensive against Cotta (Biedermann, *Gespräche,* III, 268). Obviously, this remark, taken in conjunction with the many haggling and complaining letters to Cotta, was intended to express Goethe's conviction that his publisher was getting rich at his expense. He intended, he added, to do something about that.

54. *Schillers Sohn Ernst: Eine Briefsammlung mit Einleitung von Karl Schmidt* (Paderborn, 1893), p. 289.

55. Ernst to Caroline von Wolzogen, December 31, 1827: "Hierin, muss ich gestehen, missfällt mir Goethes Betragen im hohen Grade, da er doch für seine 4,000 Rthl. an Cotta Sicherheit hat. August Goethe schreibt mir über die CorrespondenzSache einen nichtssagenden, abgeschmackten Brief, in seltsamen Vater-Goetheschen Ausdrücken, und meint, Cotta sei schwer zu behandeln, und aus der Verzögerung entspringe Gewinn. Mit Cotta ist weit besser zurecht zu kommen, als mit Goethens. Ich kann nicht leugnen, dass mir die beiden Goethe zuweilen albern erscheinen" (Schmidt, p. 322).

56. Albert Schäffle, *Cotta* (Berlin, 1895), pp. 50-54.

57. Boisserée, II, 504.

58. Schmidt, p. 330.

59. *W. A.*, IV, 44, 370.

60. This account amends and corrects an earlier article on the subject (see "Works Consulted"). The information was made available in Momme

Notes on Pages 128-129

Mommsen, *Die Entstehung von Goethes Werken* (Berlin, 1958), I, 470-529. This work will eventually make most, if not all, of the extant material on the publication of Goethe's works available in six volumes. At the time of writing only two volumes had appeared.

61. *W. A.*, IV, 46, 384.
62. *W. A.*, IV, 47, 219.
63. For a full discussion of this cf. *GJB*, XXVIII, 227, and *W. A.*, IV, 47, 290-296.

Works Consulted

Biedermann, Flodoard Freiherr von. *Die deutsche Typographie im Zeitalter Goethes.* Wien, 1928.

J. F. Unger im Verkehr mit Goethe und Schiller. Berlin, 1927.

Biedermann, Woldemar Freiherr von. *Goethe Forschungen.* Neue Folge. Leipzig, 1886.

Goethe Forschungen. Anderweite Folge. Leipzig, 1889.

Boas, Eduard. *Goethe und Schiller im Xenien-Kampf.* Stuttgart und Tübingen, 1851.

Bock, Alfred. *Aus einer kleinen Universitätsstadt.* Giessen, 1907.

Bode, Wilhelm. *Die Tonkunst in Goethes Leben.* Berlin, 1912.

Goethes Sohn. Berlin, 1918.

Böttiger, Karl August. *Literarische Zustände und Zeitgenossen,* ed. K. W. Böttiger. Leipzig, 1828.

K. A. Böttiger und G. J. Göschen im Briefwechsel, ed. L. Gerhardt. Leipzig, 1911.

Boisserée, Mathilde. *Sulpiz Boisserée.* 2 vols. Stuttgart, 1862.

Bräuning-Oktavio, Hermann. *Der Erstdruck von Goethes Götz von Berlichingen.* Darmstadt, 1923.

"Johann Heinrich Merck als Verleger," *Philobiblon,* V, Heft 1-2 (1932), 5-10; 46-52.

[Cotta, Johann Friedrich]. *Johann Friedrich Cotta zur 100. Wiederkehr seines Todestages 29. Dezember 1832.* Stuttgart, 1932.

Briefe an Cotta, ed. Maria Fehling. 3 vols. Stuttgart und Berlin, 1926-27.

Deneke, Otto. *Göttinger Beiträge zur Goethe-Bibliographie.* Göttingen, 1906-1909.

Diesch, Carl. *Bibliography of German Periodicals.* Leipzig, 1927.

Diezmann, August. *Goethe und die lustige Zeit in Weimar.* Weimar, 1926.

Düntzer, Heinrich. *Freundesbilder aus Goethes Leben.* Leipzig, 1853.

Eckermann, J. P. *Aus Goethes Lebenskreise. J. P. Eckermanns Nachlass,* ed. Friedrich Tewes. Berlin, 1905.

Enders, Karl. "Deutsche Gelegenheitsdichtung bis zu Goethe," *Germanisch-Romanische Monatsschrift,* I (1909), 292-307.

Fairley, Barker. *A Study of Goethe.* Oxford, 1947.

Feldmann, Wilhelm. *Friedrich Justin Bertuch.* Saarbrücken, 1902.

Fink, Fritz. "Friedrich Johann Justin Bertuch," *Beiträge zur Geschichte der Stadt Weimar,* Heft, 35/36, 1934.

Frankfurter gelehrte Anzeigen vom Jahr 1775. Frankfurt, 1775.

Gaedertz, Karl Theodor. *Bei Goethe zu Gaste.* Leipzig, 1900.

Geiger, Ludwig. "Die erste Ausgabe von Goethes 'Hermann und Dorothea' und ihr Verleger," *Zeitschrift für Bücherfreunde,* I, 1897/98.

Goethe, Johann Wolfgang von. *Werke.* 143 vols. Weimar, 1887-1919.

Sämtliche Werke. 41 vols. Stuttgart und Berlin, 1912.

Goethe-Jahrbuch. 34 vols. Frankfurt, 1880-1913.

Goethes Briefe an Eichstädt, ed. Woldemar Freiherr von Biedermann. Berlin, 1872.

Goethe in vertraulichen Briefen seiner Zeitgenossen, ed. Wilhelm Bode. Berlin, 1923.
Die Gesamt- und Einzeldrucke von Goethes Werken, ed. Waltraud Hagen. I. Berlin, 1953.
Goethe-Briefe aus Fritz Schlossers Nachlass, ed. Julius Frese. Stuttgart, 1877.
Briefe aus dem Freundeskreise von Goethe, Herder, Höpfner und Merck, ed. Karl Wagner. Leipzig, 1847.
Goethe-Handbuch, ed. Julius Zeitler. 3 vols. Stuttgart, 1916-18.
Schriften der Goethe-Gesellschaft. Weimar, 1885-1941.
Goldfriedrich, Johann. *Geschichte des Deutschen Buchhandels.* 4 vols. Leipzig, 1913.
Goschen, Viscount. *Goschen, Publisher and Printer.* 2 vols. New York, 1903.
Gräf, Hans G. *Goethe über seine Dichtungen.* 9 vols. Frankfurt, 1906.
Hagen, Erich von dem. *Goethe als Herausgeber von "Kunst und Alterthum" und seine Mitarbeiter.* Berlin, 1912.
Hehn, Viktor. *Gedanken über Goethe.* Berlin, 1887.
Holtei, Karl. *Vierzig Jahre.* Breslau, 1845.
Houben, H. H. *J. P. Eckermann. Sein Leben für Goethe.* 2 vols. Leipzig, 1925.
Hünich, Fritz. "Goethe und seine Verleger," *Goethe-Kalender,* 18 (1925), 99-118.
Keudell, Elise von. *Goethe als Benutzer der Weimarer Bibliothek.* Weimar, 1931.
[Knebel, K. L.] *K. L. von Knebels literarischer Nachlass und Briefwechsel,* ed. K. A. Varnhagen von Ense und Theodor Mundt. Leipzig, 1840.
Köster, Albert. "Goethe und das Publikum," *GJB,* XXIX (1908), 1*-20*.
Laistner, R. "Armbruster und die Wiener Goethe-Ausgabe," *Beilage zur Allgemeinen Zeitung,* Nr. 14, Stuttgart und München, 1894.
Loram, Ian C. "Goethe and J. F. Unger," *Germanic Review,* XXVI (April 1951), 125-135.
"Publication of the Goethe-Schiller Correspondence," *Modern Language Notes,* XLVII (June 1952), 300-304.
"Goethe's Reaction to the Pirating of his Works," *German Life and Letters,* VII (January 1954), 90-96.
"Goethe's Use of Mediators in his Publishing Activities," *German Quarterly* (January 1961), 21-27.
Markert, Karl. "Goethe und der Verlag seiner Werke," *Goethe: Neue Folge des Jahrbuchs der Goethe-Gesellschaft,* XII (1950), 144-176.
[Merck, J. H.] *Briefe an und von Johann Heinrich Merck,* ed. Karl Wagner. Darmstadt, 1838.
Mommsen, Momme. *Die Entstehung von Goethes Werken.* 2 vols. Berlin, 1958.
Morris, Max. *Der junge Goethe.* 6 vols. Leipzig, 1910.
Pusey, William. *Louis-Sebastian Mercier in Germany.* New York, 1939.
Pyritz, Hans. *Goethe-Bibliographie.* Heidelberg, 1955.
Rauscher, Otto. "Die Wiener Nachdrucke von Goethes Werken," *Chronik des Wiener Goethe-Vereins,* 40 (1935), 23-32; 41 (1936), 32-35.
"Die Wiener Originalausgabe von Goethes Werken," *Chronik des Wiener Goethe-Vereins,* 42 (1937), 37-40.
"Joseph Geistinger als Verleger Goethes," *Chronik des Wiener Goethe-Vereins,* 43 (1938), 36-37.
Rieger, Max. *Klinger in der Sturm- und Drangperiode.* Darmstadt, 1880.
Riemer, Friedrich. *Mitteilungen über Goethe.* Leipzig, 1921.
Schäffle, Albert. *Cotta.* Berlin, 1895.

161

Schiller, Friedrich von. *Sämtliche Werke.* 16 vols. Stuttgart und Berlin, 1904-05.

    Briefe, ed. Fritz Jonas. 7 vols. Stuttgart, 1892-96.

    Briefwechsel zwischen Schiller und Cotta, ed. Wilhelm Vollmer. Stuttgart, 1876.

Schmid, Günter. *Goethe und die Naturwissenschaften.* Eine Bibliographie. Halle, 1940.

    Schicksal einer Goetheschrift. Burg Giebichenstein, 1937.

Schmidt, Erich. *Heinrich Leopold Wagner.* Jena, 1879.

    Lenz und Klinger, Zwei Dichter der Geniezeit. Berlin, 1878.

Sondheim, Moritz. *Die Gestalt der Schriften Goethes im Wandel der Zeit.* Frankfurt, 1932.

Soret, Frédéric. *Conversations avec Goethe.* Paris, 1932.

Steinhilber, Hans-Dieter. *Goethe als Vertragspartner von Verlagen.* (Diss.) Hamburg, 1960.

Vaternahm, Otto. *Goethe und seine Verleger.* Heidelberg, 1916.

Witkowski, Georg. "Goethe und seine Verleger," *Börsenblatt,* 72 (1906), 2676-2683.

Wolzogen, Caroline von. *Literarischer Nachlass der Frau Caroline von Wolzogen,* ed. B. Abeken. 2 vols. Leipzig, 1848.

Index

Schiller on, 123; Wilhelm von Humboldt's part in negotiations for, 123; payment for, 123; Ernst von Schiller duns G. for payment for, 123; August von Goethe rejects Ernst's request, 123; Ernst threatens court action over, 123; G. demands cash on delivery for, 124; Cotta's reaction to G.'s demand, 124-27; G.'s angry response, 127-28; Ernst von Schiller investigates problem of payment for, 128; misunderstanding about, 128; G. sends MS to Cotta, 128; G.'s attitude toward Cotta over, 159n53; Ernst von Schiller's annoyance with G. over, 159n55; mentioned, 89, 90

—Individual works: *Annette*, 2; *Aufgeregten, Die*, 154n7; *Benvenuto Cellini*, 57-58, 60, 131; *Beobachtungen und Betrachtungen über Gegenstände aus der Naturgeschichte und Naturlehre*, 42; *Brief des Pastors . . .*, 7; *Bürgergeneral, Der*, 39, 40; *Claudine von Villa Bella*, 12; *Clavigo*, 8, 9; *Dichtung und Wahrheit*, 1, 8, 9, 68, 69-70, 74, 75, 77, 81, 92, 116, 131, 134, 156n14; *Elpenor*, 63; *Erwin und Elmire*, 11-12, 13, 105; *Faust*, 44, 56, 58, 109, 121; *Fischerin, Die*, 12; *Geschichte Gottfriedens von Berlichingen, dramatisiert*, 5; *Götter, Helden und Wieland*, 8, 10; *Götz von Berlichingen*, 6, 8, 9, 10, 14, 105; *guten Frauen, Die*, 155n28; *Hermann und Dorothea*, 10, 26, 33, 35, 44, 45, 48-51, 155n21; *Iphigenie*, 14, 19, 20, 37, 40, 154n3; *Italienische Reise*, 14, 74, 77; *Jahrmarkts-fest zu Plundersweilern, Das*, 7-8; *Jery und Bätely*, 12; *Leiden des jungen Werthers, Die*, 8, 9, 14, 20, 105, 152n18; *Mahomet*, 57; *Maskenzüge*, 32; *Metamorphose der Pflanzen, Die*, 25-26, 28, 48, 130, 153n46; *Mitschuldigen, Die*, 2, 3, 151, 151n3; *natürliche Tochter, Die*, 47, 58; *Neueröffnetes moralischpolitisches Puppenspiel*, 7; *Organische Bildung*, 77; *Philip Hackert*, 68-69; *Prolog zu den neuesten Offenbarungen Gottes*, 9-10; *Rameaus Neffe*, 78;

Römische Carneval, Das, 37-38, 48; *Römische Elegien*, 34; *Satyros*, 9; *Scherz, List und Rache*, 12; *Singspiele*, 11-12, 14, 15; *Stella*, 10-11, 19; *Tag- und Jahreshefte*, 93; *Tasso*, 14, 21, 24, 154n3; *Über Kunst und Alterthum*, 34, 121; *Venetianische Epigramme*, 34; *Vögel, Die*, 12; *Vorspiel für Halle*, 74; *Vorspiele*, 32; *Wahlverwandtschaften, Die*, 29, 67, 68, 72, 105; *Was wir bringen*, 57, 58, 76; *West-östliche Divan, Der*, 78-79, 87; *Wilhelm Meisters Lehrjahre*, 62, 135, 154n9, 154n11, 154n34; *Wilhelm Meisters Theatralische Sendung*, 14, 15; *Wilhelm Meisters Wanderjahre*, 34, 68, 69, 79, 159n-47; *Wissenschaftliche Schriften*, 34; *Xenien*, 43; *Zauberflöte, Zweyter Theil, Der*, 155n28; *Zur Farbenlehre*, 67-68; *Zur Morphologie*, 151n3; *Zwo wichtige . . . Biblische Fragen*, 7, 151n12

—Mediator: pattern of mediation, 29; Bertuch as, 29; Schiller as, 29, 106-10, 158n27; Boisserée as, 107, 159n43; for individual works, 80; use of, 104-11; reasons for use of, 158n29

—Piracy: unconcern about, 3-4; admits problem of, 73; reactions to, 91-101; Viennese edition of collected works, 156n15; ruling in Vienna against, 156n21

—*Propyläen, Die*: advice to Cotta about, 54-55; reaction to failure of, 55, 56-57; Cotta's financial problems with, 155n25; mentioned, 78, 109, 116

—Relationship with Cotta. 52-160 *passim;* discussions with, 53-54; impression of, 53-54; priority to, 56; first contract with, 58; first edition of collected works published by, 60-66, C.'s conditions for, 60, payment for, 61, G.'s instructions for printing of, 62; G.'s criticism of, 62-63; C. offers advance on, 63-64; G.'s lack of enthusiasm for, 65-66; G.'s impatience over, 66; problem of dating, 66; individual works published by, 66-70; summary of early years of association with, 69; second edition of collected works published by, 70-78; C. broaches subject of, 70; G.'s reservations about, 70; reasons for disagreement over, 71; G.'s blunt statement about, 72; G. admits misunderstanding about, 72; G.'s vagueness about, 73; C. visits G. to discuss, 73; remuneration for, 75-76; C. agrees to G.'s terms for, 76; G.'s proposal concerning, 76; G.'s difficulty in filling out, 77-78; completion of, 78; collected works as basis for defining G.-C. relationship, 81-82; third edition of collected works published by, 83-160 *passim* (*Ausgabe letzter Hand*); G. hints about, 83; C. suggests publication of, 84; G.'s friends help with, 84; discussion of payment for, 89-90; G. avoids immediate negotiations for, 90; G. about to sign contract for, 100; neglected because of copyright problem, 101; C.'s willingness to publish, 101; G.'s complaint about C.'s inactivity over, 101; bids from other publishers for, 101-2; Joseph Max makes offer for, 102; C. declares interest in, 102; G. demands offer from C. for, 103; C. wishes to have intermediary for, 104; offer by Reimer for, 104; G. suggests Boisserée as mediator for, 104; as bequest to family, 111; G.'s plans for, 112; C.'s suggestions for payment for, 112-13; August von Goethe's suggestion for payment for, 112; C.'s opinion of August's suggestion, 112; G.'s decision to sign with C. for, 113-14; G. renews subject of higher payment for, 114; Boisserée's opinion of G.'s demands, 114; C. agrees to G.'s terms for, 114; G. again hesitates to sign for, 114; G. reopens negotiations for, 115-16; C.'s reaction to G.'s demands, 115; G. still refuses to reveal other bids for, 116-17; G.'s distrust of C.'s motives, 116; C.'s final offer for, 117-18; G. accepts final offer for, 118; G. again refuses to disclose other offers for, 118-19; C. and G. express mutual satisfaction over, 118; G. concerned over C.'s slowness in beginning, 119-20; G. sends C. mate-

rial for, 119; G.'s interest in physical aspect of, 119; rumor of Viennese edition of, 120; G.'s suspicions about C., 120; G. refuses to allow changes in, 120-21; C.'s problems with, 121; C. hurt by G.'s announcement about, 121-22; G. agrees to changes in, 122; slow publication of, 128-29; C. asks G. to get Dutch copyright for, 129; G. requests Luxembourg copyright for, 129; last piracy problem with, 129; summary of G.'s relationship with C., 130-33, 137-39. *See also* Cotta
—Relationship with Göschen: first authorized edition of G.'s collected works, 14-25; reasons for negotiating with Göschen, 15, 16; demands on Göschen, 16-17; Göschen agrees to G.'s terms, 17; demands for payment, 18; G. underestimates task of editing, 18; instructions for Göschen, 18-19; G. distracted in Italy, 20; G.'s determination to fulfil contract, 20; public apathy toward edition, 21; G. displeased with edition, 22; G.'s interpretation of contract with Göschen, 28; mellowed opinion of Göschen, 28; summary of relations with Göschen, 29-31, 136-37; confusion about Unger and Göschen, 152n27
—Relationship with Unger: 35-48; Moritz as intermediary for *Neue Schriften*, 36; G.'s attitude toward U., 36-37; remuneration for *Neue Schriften*, 38; payment for *Wilhelm Meisters Lehrjahre*, 38; lack of contract for *Neue Schriften*, 38-39; *Neue Schriften* not edition of collected works, 39; G. offers U. part of *Optische Beyträge*, 39; publication of *Reineke Fuchs*, 39-40; G.'s criticism of U., 41; G. permits U. to publish *Wilhelm Meisters Lehrjahre*, 41; U. requests permission to use "*Fraktur*," 41-42; *Wilhelm Meisters Lehrjahre* published, 42; G.'s sovereign attitude toward U., 42; U. presses G. for material, 43, 44, 45; Vieweg uses title of *Neue Schriften*, 45; G.'s instructions for U., 45-46; last volume of *Neue Schriften*, 46; G. embarrassed by U., 47; G.'s feelings

brings G. and Cotta together, 52;
characterizes G. for Cotta, 56; in-
termediary between G. and Cotta,
60; collected works of, 61; warns
Cotta about G., 72; as mediator,
104, 106-10; posthumous edition
of works, 121-22; mentioned, 38,
43, 44, 50, 53, 54, 57, 74, 80. *See
also* Goethe, *sub* Mediator
Schlosser, J. G., 8
Schmieder, C. G., 25
Schubarth, K. E., 84
Schuckmann, F. von, 100, 148
Schultz, C. F. L., 83, 84, 88, 156n2
Seidel, P., 19, 20, 24
Stein, Charlotte von, 15, 17, 29
Stolberg, Auguste von, 4

Tieck, Ludwig, 78

Unger, Friederike, 155n16
Unger, Johann Friedrich: association
with G., 35-48; mentioned, 27, 29,
50, 53, 62, 82, 154n15. *See also*

Goethe, *sub* Relationship with
Unger

Vieweg, Friedrich: relationship with
G., 43-51 *passim;* G.'s feelings to-
wards, 137; mentioned, 10, 11,
32, 33, 44, 53, 82, 155n21. *See
also* Goethe, *sub* Relationship with
Vieweg
Vulpius, Christian August, 64, 155n5
Vulpius, Christiane, 64

Weimar: G's first publications in,
12-14; occupation of, 64; possibility of plundering of, 68; G.'s
attitude after arrival in, 135
Weygand, C. F., 7, 8, 105
Wieland, Christoph Martin: assists
G. with editing, 17; *Musarion,* 52;
mentioned, 8, 34, 64
Wolzogen, Caroline von, 123

Zauper, J. S., 84
Zelter, Friedrich, 35, 47, 66, 67,
100
Zimmermann, J. G., 9

168